SILENT
SCREAM

SILENT
SCREAM

THE "INSIDE" STORY

BY VICKI CHERRY

XULON PRESS

Xulon Press
2301 Lucien Way #415
Maitland, FL 32751
407.339.4217

www.xulonpress.com

Unless otherwise indicated, Scripture quotations taken from (Version(s) used)

Printed in the United States of America

Paperback ISBN-13: 978-1-6322-1667-0
Ebook ISBN-13: 978-1-6322-1668-7

This book is dedicated to
everyone I ever loved, or hated…befriended, or rejected…
admired, or despised…
forgave … or couldn't for a while.
What I did to you, I did to me…for we are one, for we are
all the same.
So be happy, or sad…angry, or kind…forgiving, or not.

We each have a choice.

We can choose to be part of the problem in our world,
or we can be healed, and become part of the solution.

TABLE OF CONTENTS

INTRODUCTION

How DO you write a book, anyway? I understand how others do it, with outlines, and organization, and quiet time to absorb into the "spirit" of a work. I don't have any formal training in this area, nor do I seem to have much of what I would blissfully regard as quiet time, but I do have some experiences to share, so I will simply let God unfold the story, much as He has unfolded my life, with the most heart-opening surprises around every corner. I can only pray that this effort will help others to understand what's available to them, as children of the Most High God.

First, of course, we'll need a little background, but please understand that this is the part of my life BEFORE I was awakened to the reality of God, and the power to heal that He carries.

In the first part of this book I'm going to introduce you to a crippled human being. That would be me. Oh, I don't mean crippled in the physical sense of the word. By crippled, I mean emotionally, psychologically, and spiritually crippled. I've come to realize that this crippling was something that I would have to experience, with all of it's pain and embarrassment, in order to seek healing, receive healing, and hopefully be able to lead others to the very source of healing that I found. By introducing you to the life and interpretations of this crippled human being, I hope to shed a little light on what a "sinner" really is. I believe that God sees the mistakes (sins) of the crippled in a light of understanding that we have only gotten a glimpse of, if we've been blessed. And if we'reTRULY blessed, we've been that cripple who has met Him in that light.

The end of this story cannot be written yet, of course, for it is about my life, and obviously my time in this world has not yet expired, any more than has my learning adventure. However, I will close it by showing how this former "cripple" has become a confident, happy and "empowered" human being with a positive new outlook on life. Everything in between is an account of how I got here.

If you can identify with the person in the first part of this story, and you find that's where you are, get excited! There's a way out! I know, because I found it.

If you've been where I was, and you've experienced your own healings, then pray that this book falls into the hands of those who haven't. You and I together will be partners in guiding others out of pain.

If you grew up happy and secure, and you've found yourself condemning others who just keep making a mess of their lives, my hope is that this book will shed enough light on bad behavior that you'll be able to throw off those religious robes of self-righteousness, roll your spiritual sleeves up, and get to work on helping them heal. Your prayers, from an understanding heart, will be sufficient.

And Jesus said to me, "Who art thou, oh man, to criticize another, for who amongst you knows upon whom I will bestow My Spirit tomorrow?"

chapter 1
THE KID

I entered this world destined to be the only child of an alcoholic father and mother who was what's referred to these days as "emotionally unavailable". My mother lived in a prison of her own fears which kept her from venturing out into the world with me, to introduce me to life in any way, other than the one she was bound to, but isn't that generally the case? My father, equally unavailable, lived in an emotional prison of his own, which had been constructed from twisted memories of his own abusive childhood. My parents both suffered from varying degrees of anxiety, although they dealt with their fear of life in totally opposite ways. My mother hid within the confines of her own imagination, ritualistically performing her daily household chores, while my father hid in clubs and bars, which provided him the escape he needed from the routine my mother found so satisfying. My mother faithfully walked me up the street to a fundamental church as I was growing up and, except for an occasional visit with relatives, we spent the rest of our time in a monotonously silent home. My father, having no desire to mix lifestyles, never attended church with us, but chose instead to remain in bed on Sunday mornings to nurse whatever degree of misery his social life had inflicted on him the night before.

I've heard that my parents had a reasonably good relationship in the first few years of marriage, but then I came along. I was told that I was a highly desired addition to the family in my mother's eyes. Her plan was to have more than one child, though. In her eyes a lot of children was what constituted a real family. She had wanted children from the beginning, but it would be five years before I would make my debut. My father, on the other hand, wasn't quite as excited about my arrival as my mother. Apparently the negative impact that his own childhood had made on him had caused him to reject the very thought of childhood in all of it's forms, including me.

My mother and father, for the most part, constituted my world. Thus, as I was growing up, my world consisted of tip-toeing around a father who terrified me, and keeping a watchful eye on my mother, who never realized that I would have need of actual communication skills, so we rarely talked. If my dad spoke to me at all, he addressed me as "Hey, Kid…", and if he referred to me in any way in a statement to anyone else, he referred to me as "The Kid". In all of my life, he never called me by my name. I'm not sure that he'd been told that I had one. He didn't seem to have a problem talking to other people, but when it came to me, it was as though I were an object rather than a person. My mother, on the other hand, may never have carried on a meaningful conversation with me, but she did have a pet name for me. I was, as she would often tell me, her little "Vicki Girl," and somehow I knew she loved me.

The closest she ever got toward a heart-to-heart conversation with me was to tell me during my first marriage that she was sorry that she'd never talked to me much while I was growing up, but that she had considered me to be her little shadow following her around the house, and that had made her happy, just knowing that I was there.

My parents were so mismatched, that I'm sure my mother needed me there to help fill the void of loneliness in her life, even though it appeared that it was my arrival that had ruined everything. I would hear her tell others that they had been happy before I was born, but that after I'd come along, my dad had started leaving the house more and more, as if he couldn't stand being around me. I was embarrassed about that. Even as a child, I knew by the things I overheard, that my being born was not a good thing. My father, who had viewed my birth as an intrusion, used my presence as an excuse for spending more time in town, a habit that would increase over the years, as would the monster that was living inside him.

I was always nervous around my dad. He hated me, but for the sake of my mother, he tolerated me. I think he just didn't know what to do with me. My mother, on the other hand, although she had wanted me in her life desperately, couldn't seem to figure out what to do with me, either. She could only do with me the things that her fearful restrictions would allow, and that wasn't much. We didn't go to any school functions, or anywhere else outside the home, save that occasional visit with a relative, for she just couldn't imagine going anywhere without my dad. She was just too afraid. Since his favorite off-the-job interests were generally found in bars, which didn't include us, mom and I stayed home. My mother spent my childhood years waiting for my dad, and I learned to spend those years trying to avoid him. The longer my mother waited, the more withdrawn she became at home, and the more withdrawn she became, the lonelier I got. I didn't dare get close to my father because he terrified me, and I couldn't break through the prison walls my mother lived behind, so I was always on the outside, and always alone.

I've seen people's reactions many times over the years when it would come out in conversation that I was an "only child". There's a judgment that accompanies that label. The common assumption is that the only child is the spoiled brat, the apple of their parents' eyes, the one who's been showered with too much attention, and the one who's never learned to share. In my case, the only part of that that was true, was the fact that I never learned to share. We lived in poverty because of my father's habits, so I didn't really HAVE much of anything to share as far as material things were concerned. I would much rather have "shared" than to not have had anyone to share WITH, which was more the case. The biggest problem for me was that I never learned to share thoughts, dreams, hope, or love… a much more important "sharing" than toys could ever be.

When there were family gatherings, I generally opted to remain in my mother's company. I would plant myself by my mother's side, to the dismay of the other adults. The habit of being invisibly "glued" to my mother, I had adopted as a survival tactic. My mother, in order not to bring upon herself the disapproval of the others, would express HER disapproval at my stubborn refusal to "just go and play with the other kids!" But by her side I would remain, and I have no idea how many grown-up conversations I squelched during those years, but I know I did. The circumstances had created for my mother the very thing that made her happy. I was her shadow.

I'll guarantee that I was a topic of conversation many times because of this, but it would only have been people wondering why I was such a weird and backward child. I actually FELT like a weird kid, and I FELT the disapproval of the others, but that wasn't enough to make me change my ways. I had found a way to survive, and I was going to stick with it, no matter what. My loyalty to my mother, born out of fear, she interpreted as devotion, and she basked in the glow of all that love. I, on the other hand, remaining steadfast in my determination to remain safe, had to tolerate the weight of the judgments, both spoken and unspoken, of those who never understood my dilemma.

I don't criticize my parents any more, although I did for many years after I grew up. I know now that they had some pretty awful demons to deal with in their own lives, but that didn't stop me from growing up frustrated and angry, because I DIDN'T understand that then. All I knew was that I was a nonentity. A misfit. I was a very lonely person, but I didn't realize at the time what that awful feeling was that was always in me. And I was always afraid. I was afraid of being left alone, and even more afraid of having to be with people. I was afraid of never being noticed, and terrified that I would be. I had no sense of belonging, so I had none of the confidence that a person has when they know that they belong. I knew there was something wrong with me, but it would take years for me to figure it out. What was wrong was that I hadn't bonded with anyone, or if I had, that bond had been broken very early in my life.

I know people believed, as I did, that there was a strong bond between me and my mother, but I've come to realize that there's a significant difference between a bond between people and just plain clinging. A bond is born of love and trust, while clinging is a result of fear, an act of desperation.

chapter 2
THE SCREAM

I grew up with something inside me that I've come to refer to as a "silent scream". This condition exists in those of us who've grown up in a hostile environment, whether it's blatantly hostile, or subtly, like mine. The greatest emotional or psychological pain that a person can carry is the feeling that they don't belong, for belonging carries with it a sense of safety, which I never had. I had carried this pain of not belonging for as long as I could remember. I couldn't identify it, of course, let alone explain it. I just felt it. I lived in a world of quiet longing. A longing that someone else might sense the danger in that house, and rescue me. No one ever did, though, so I discovered my own kind of hiding place.

There is a place of inner solitude that we retreat to if we've been wounded, and apparently I had discovered this place as a very young child, entered it, felt safe there, and decided to stay. The "sanctuary of aloneness" as I've heard it described since, is a very lonely dwelling place indeed, but since it feels safer to remain there than to venture out to be exposed to the predators in this world, it seems to be the lesser of the two evils, and so we stay. I say "we" because there are many invisible prisons like the one I lived in, each housing a very precious child of God, with a very special purpose. This sanctuary is inhabited by those of us who have condemned ourselves to a distorted and unlovable self-image, in agreement with those who, although they may have loved us, lacked the ability to convey love properly.

Within the walls of this invisible prison, I pretended that I'd be okay, and since there was no one else inside those walls to tell me otherwise, I survived in that place for a very long time. Some spend their entire lifetimes there. It's sad, really, because it is a painfully empty existence rather than a life. The longer I stayed there, the more damage was done to me, and worse yet, as time went on, to others around me.

I became a studier of people, especially during my school years. I'd be caught rudely staring at people from time to time, which was embarrassing, and seemed to make them uncomfortable, but I wasn't trying to make anyone uncomfortable. I was simply searching for a key to "normalcy". I never knew when I would discover this key, or who it was that had it, but I was sure that someone carried the answer that I needed, and so I watched others intently.

I was fascinated by happy people. I wondered what it was that made them feel so good about themselves, but I was much too shy to ask, no matter how badly I wanted to know what made them so different from me. There were a few times when a "normal" person would get dangerously close to me in my hiding place, and even attempt to strike up a conversation with me, at which times I would become nervously tongue-tied and end up saying something stupid. Humiliated, I would retreat to an even deeper place in my inner solitude, which would ensure that no one would be able to notice me THIS time and no one else would see how pathetic I was. Talk about a living hell! Anyone who's ever lived in this hellish place would have to agree that that's exactly what it is.

The worst part is, we can't come out because we're terrified, but we're so lonely, we'd give most anything if someone could come along and release us. The frustration of the situation creates the "silent scream". "PLEASE, COULD SOMEBODY HELP ME!! PLEASE! I'M DYING IN HERE!! PLEASE!!! I DON'T WANT TO BE DIFFERENT! I WANT TO BE LIKE EVERYBODY ELSE, BUT I DON'T KNOW HOW! PLEASE HELP ME! I'M SOOOOOO SCARED!!"

Oh, the sadness of a scream that isn't heard. We're so afraid of being discovered that we don't dare allow the scream to come out of our mouths. THAT would only serve to reveal our vulnerability, and THAT might bring more humiliation. But the silence of the scream becomes the loudest part of our existence, and it begins eventually to seep out in forms of behavior that only give evidence to what we suspected all along. There's something desperately WRONG with us!

chapter 3
HOPE DIES QUIETLY

In the beginning, I know I made the same playful noises that any child would make in the everyday task of entertaining myself. It never seemed to fail, though, that I would find myself being sharply ridiculed by my dad for whatever noise I had come up with for the occasion, be it talking, giggling, or singing. He would end every criticism with an additional comment on how stupid I was. I would become instantly shamed by his cruel comments, wishing I had never made the noise in the first place. I never knew what I was doing wrong, but I knew I'd done SOMETHING wrong so I worked hard at curbing the natural expressions of childhood. I kept the giggles and the talking and the singing inside as much as possible. They were still there, but I wouldn't let them escape as easily as I had done before. I learned from my father that self-expression could lead to humiliation, so being less spontaneous was a much safer way to go. I learned to be very self-controlled because of him. Now, self-control is a GOOD thing, but it should be taught by example. It just hurts when it's taught by shame.

I would cringe at the look in my father's eyes when he criticized me. I hated his eyes even more than the criticism. The look in his eyes told me I was disgusting. This just made me feel worse, because the man hated me, and I had no way to get away from him. I just wished that I could be quiet enough, that he'd forget that I was there. If he didn't notice me, he couldn't hurt me, right? WRONG! I tried the "out of sight, out of mind" technique over the years. Maybe, I thought, if I stayed out of his sight, he'd forget about me, and forget to fence me in with his daily restrictions. That plan never worked, either. If he didn't see me, he'd simply convey the list of restrictions to my mother FOR me. And once he had spoken, his word was law, and I hated his law. It was a "Law of Emptiness", from which there was no escape.

Outwardly, I became a quietly composed, polite, and soft spoken person. Inwardly, I seethed with hatred at the way I lived. I wasn't allowed to go with other kids. I wasn't permitted to go to a friend's house after school. No one could come to my house after school, because my dad was always out nights, and would often sleep on the sofa during the day. I always had to be too quiet to be able to have friends over, unless my dad wasn't home, but then you were taking a big chance, because what if he'd forgotten something, and came back? I wasn't allowed out of the house after dark, which made life very difficult during the winter months, when it was already dark by five o'clock in the afternoon.

When my dad said you didn't go out after dark, he meant not even onto the front porch. His limitless supply of daily restrictions, such as "don't leave the house today, don't leave the porch, don't go down the street, don't have anyone here, just stay in your room today…" would pierce my heart like disappointed shock waves. He became so ridiculous about the restrictions, that eventually my mother would feel sorry enough for me that she'd let me go up the street to a neighbor's house for a while, once she was assured that he was gone for the night.

I loved it when he left each evening. I'd watch him going down the steps from our apartment, and listen for the door to close. Then I'd wait for the sound of the car starting. Only after I heard the sound of the car leaving, would I begin to breathe. There were times, though, when I'd anticipate his leaving, knowing that I'd finally be able to relax my guard, and he'd yell back up the steps to my mother, "Oh, and tell the kid not to leave the house today." I would deflate like a pin-popped balloon. I wouldn't actually have any plans anyway, but once the king had spoken, it was as good as engraved on my tombstone, and if anything DID come up to do, it was guaranteed already that I would not be the one doing it. And I would silently scream inside "WHY?"

I grew up wondering just exactly what it was that I was always being punished for. Had my mother been a more verbal person, she might have balanced my world a little by confronting him about the things he would say to me, or she might have at least told me that the things he said weren't true, but at home she wasn't very expressive, so her silence, accompanied by her pitying glance, was a signal to me that this truly was my fate, and that I'd have no choice but to do as I was told. And that's exactly what I did. I had been told I was stupid for so long, that when I did find the courage to assert myself in any way, whatever I chose to do would invariably turn out to be something stupid.

By the time I was fifteen years old, the years of my dad's subtle cruelties had created in me a self-loathing, non-essential, totally confused and shame-filled creature who, in order to have any life at all, would have to sneak and lie, and then feel guilty about THAT because, don't forget, I was being raised in a fundamental church, and God didn't tolerate a sneak, or a liar. I'd heard about love, but what I had experienced was hate. After a few years of living in this defeating situation, I figured I wasn't good enough for God's world, either. The scream inside was becoming nearly deafening by now.

chapter 4
TERROR

I don't know if my father was an acting-out child molester in the first few years of my life, but I suspect now that he was, due to the fact that I had been afraid of him as long as I could remember. However, by the time I was eight years old, I knew for a fact that he was. The reason I think the problem had cropped up earlier than when I was eight, was because of a particular day when I was younger that made me wonder later what was really wrong in that house, even back then.

I had gotten up in the morning and sneaked quietly past my dad, who was sleeping on the sofa in the living room, to get to the kitchen to let my mother know that I was up for the day. She wasn't there, so I slipped silently back past him to go and check in their bedroom. She wasn't there either. We lived in a small, second-floor apartment, so it wasn't like there were many places to be, and it was her natural routine to be in the kitchen in the mornings, so what was wrong here? I tip-toed back into the living room, so I wouldn't wake my dad, and then I saw something that terrified me. Her housecoat and pajamas were neatly hanging over the back of the chair in the corner. This was not a normal thing for this woman to do. She had a routine for her life that you could set a clock by. Oh, no! She's gone!

I can still remember the horror that I felt go through me when I thought my mother had left me there. She was my safety in this house. I quietly crawled into the corner behind that chair to hide, my heart pounding like a terrified animal, and silently slipped her clothes down from the back of the chair, and sobbed into her housecoat, never allowing a sound to escape, and never taking my eyes off my dad lying there on the sofa. He was the one I feared.

I had to be quiet, so he wouldn't wake up. "Mom, please don't leave me here with him. PLEASE don't leave me here with him!" I kept screaming into the housecoat. It was an actual scream inside, but it came out in the form of a whisper, which I didn't permit to get past the housecoat pressed tightly against my mouth. "What did I do wrong? Please come back and get me! I PROMISE I'll be good! I'll do anything you want, just PLEASE DON'T LEAVE ME HERE WITH HIM!"

I was discovered behind that chair when my mother returned. She'd probably not been gone longer than an hour, although it had felt like an eternity to me. I was so thrilled to know that she wasn't gone forever, that when asked what I was doing behind the chair, I beamed as I answered "I was just hiding to surprise you."

As it turned out, she had only gone to see someone who was sick. She hadn't really left me there alone with him after all. I never told anyone what I was really doing behind the chair. There was no need, and we never talked about things like that anyway. I was about five years old at the time that happened, and I still remember every detail as though it happened yesterday. That's what terror does. It hits you with such impact, that it refuses to be forgotten.

I'm not saying that I had numerous improper times of having to be alone with this man, but the few times I was a victim, on top of the way I already felt about myself, were unbearable to say the least. I've often wondered, since I've gotten older, if maybe he DID know that he had a serious problem, and that's why he didn't want to have any kids, and maybe that's why he'd acted so strangely toward me from the beginning, but since we never talked, I'd never know.

I'm always thrilled to hear these days that children are being openly taught to get away from people that scare them, or make them feel bad inside. What I'm talking about though, are the people who really CAN'T get away from the predators, because the predators are living in their homes, and even worse, they're the authority in those homes. The only way to stop the predators is to expose them. I was taught to be silent, so I was able to be a victim and so were others. Then, because they also didn't say anything, more victims would surely have been made.

You might wonder how it is that these things happen, and some children still don't say anything even when they are taught now that they should tell somebody. Why DO some of them just curl up inside and try to die rather than tell someone and get safe? If they're made to feel like bad people beforehand, they don't feel they have the right to complain about anything that happens to them. They've already been conditioned for abuse. If, like me, they feel guilty that they were even born, they're not going to be demanding a fair and happy life. Instead, they'll stifle all natural tendencies, and stuff the shame down deep inside, and silently scream "WHY?"

chapter 5
A SPLIT DECISION

There is a very diabolical phenomenon that takes place in the person who has experienced this type of deep, dark wounding. The child we were, in all of our innocent trusting, splits away from our outer person, and hides away in pain while on the outside we are growing up just like anyone else. I've heard, and read, of people describing the condition of the child who's been molested or raped as being someone who's been robbed of their innocence, and that's what I used to believe, but I know now that's not completely true. If we have been robbed of innocence, then it's gone. Someone has stolen it. But I came to find out that that is not really the case. The innocence that we had is not gone at all, for the innocence IS who we are, in the form of a child who lives within us, who's been wounded or terrorized, and has crawled away deep within us, to hide. And this little person hurts so bad, but we aren't even aware that they are in there. All we know is that we hurt inside, deep inside. So we, without knowing what's really going on, set out to find something to ease the pain.

I lived for the day when I could leave home, and get away from not only my dad, who had hated me since birth, and had molested me as though I wasn't real, but my mother, who never knew what he was really like and waited on him like a servant. And the day comes when we're able to leave this prison that the rest of the world calls "home", and our joy knows no bounds. Maybe we'll have a chance at life after all, once we get away from these people. We determine that we will leave this place, and leave these circumstances, and leave the pain behind. Enter, the irony.

Without realizing it, we've come into agreement with these people. We believe that there was something wrong with this kid that we were, too, or it wouldn't have been so hard for people to love us. We subconsciously believe that the child we were was disgusting, or so pathetic that we are only to be pitied, for that's the message we were given, so now we reject that child, too. We don't want to be that weird person that nobody cared about, so we deny the existence of the child we were, our true self, and we stuff ourselves into a more acceptable mold. We try to become someone that others won't be so intolerant of. And we carry pain inside. We don't know yet that the pain inside is the pain of who we really are, desperately wounded, and needing to be loved, wanting to be recognized, but fearing further harm. We have now become our own worst nightmare. We will not allow the true self to be seen, let alone loved. We are too ashamed of who we really are, because we were so criticized when we were just being ourselves. We didn't know that it was their wounds, rather than our flaws, that caused this.

We do whatever it takes to fit in, because we can't tolerate any more criticism. We become actors, accepting the approval of the audience, in place of real love. We wear our "stage make-up" for so long that even WE begin to think that's who we really are, but it isn't. It never was. We have become entertainers, rather than who God intended us to be.

We want to be rid of the pain, so we do whatever we think it will take to get rid of it. And so we walk the child inside of us through one abusive situation after another with the unconscious intention of finishing the job that the parent, or parents, had begun. Once and for all, we're going to destroy that pain, but to destroy the pain is to destroy the child inside, so we unknowingly begin our mission to self-destruct.

I didn't know, when I left home, that that was what was going on with me. I just thought I was changing my life now, and thought that I'd be happy. I married a twenty year old alcoholic when I was sixteen years old. We were nothing more than two children, both products of alcoholic homes, who had no idea what a normal marriage consisted of. Neither of us had developed any real communication skills, so we lived together in the same house, in our separate prisons, neither of us having any idea how to be successful at anything, let alone a relationship. We lasted only four years. We had two beautiful children during those four years, but neither of us knew, from what we had experienced, how to break the self-destructive patterns that we had both developed. And neither of us knew how to find the kind of love that is forever... the kind of love that heals.

chapter 6
YOU LIVE WHAT YOU LEARN

Although I felt safer around my mother while growing up, she never shared with me who she was, but she taught me what she knew. By her example, she taught me things like how to take pride in my work, and how to do it RIGHT, and how to keep things to myself. From my father I learned card games and shame, frustration, humiliation, and rage. In his own twisted way, he had also taught me everything HE knew.

As I said earlier, my dad was an alcoholic, and I know now why people drink. It helps to numb the emotional pain they carry. I know, because there was a period in my life when I did the same. Alcohol is a double-minded friend, however, who soothes you for a moment, while coaxing you into even worse situations that will bring about even more pain than you had before. Then, when the greater pain is felt, it takes even more alcohol to numb our panicked conscience, and on and on it goes, until we find ourselves on a roller coaster ride of alcoholism that has no shut-off switch. The most we can hope for is a crash at the end of the ride. My ride lasted for about a ten- year period.

We run over so many people on that ride, but we build up so much speed that we probably didn't even see them standing there, let alone know we've crushed them. Every now and then we get a glimpse of someone else's pain that we have caused, but before we can go back and try to do anything about it, we're zipping around the next loop at a breakneck speed and the person we crushed is left behind in our race ahead to even more painful experiences. The guilt we carry because we saw them getting hurt is too horrible to bear, so we drink to bring ourselves to a greater state of oblivion, for we are unable to deal with their pain any more than we were able to deal with our own. We tell ourselves that they will be all right, but deep down we fear they won't, so there's another reason to drink. To dull the pain of guilt for what we've done.

Alcohol is a very cruel pain-killer indeed, for it opens the door to a multitude of mistakes that can traumatize another person for life, most of all the very people that we loved, but couldn't communicate that love to properly. In my father's case, it had opened the door to perversions which not only myself, but others, fell victim to. I despised my father while I was growing up because I was so afraid of him. Just being around him made me feel bad. I came to realize much later in life that I had hated my mother too, without even realizing it, for not protecting me from him. But then, how could she have known, when I never told her, but I never told her, because we didn't talk. I hated her for living with my dad, but I couldn't tell her that. You never express anger against the only one who's presence keeps you safe. She hadn't intentionally abandoned me to this man, but in her own naïve way, had done just that. It could never have occurred to her that such a diabolical entity could be living in her house. She simply didn't think that way.

chapter 7
PASSING ON THE PAIN

Growing up in a void is hardly proper preparation for becoming a wife or parent. A person who's been emotionally crippled, needs to be healed and stabilized before they can take on the responsibility of others in ANY kind of relationship. Of course, I didn't know any of this when I got married. I didn't know much of anything about ANYTHING, so I entered into marriage with only one pattern in my mind, and that was the pattern my parents had set before me. I imagined that I would cook and clean and do laundry, and my husband would go out to make the money to pay the bills, and somehow everything would just magically work! Talk about naïve.

Did I love my husband? Yes, to the best of my disability, I really did. However, I knew absolutely nothing about successful relationships, and what it took to develop them, so I played the same role of housewife that I had seen my mother play. It hadn't made for a happy home when I was growing up, but I fell into the same pattern, for lack of having any other, and guess what? You're right, it didn't work any better this time. While I concentrated on having a spotless house, just like my mom had done, and making sure meals were ready on time, just like mom, my husband went out more and more, just like my dad had done. I didn't want to live like my parents had lived, but we were LIVING it. We separated after four years of copying our parents.

I raised my kids in the same emotional void that I had been raised in because, once again, I copied the pattern that had been set before me. I hadn't been taught any parenting skills, and after having been convinced for years that I was hopelessly stupid, I automatically curbed my natural mothering instincts too, on the advice of an older woman, another well-meaning emotional cripple who insisted that I not hold my children much, because, she said, it would "spoil" them. Since I didn't trust my own judgment on anything, I sadly adhered to the advice of this woman, assuming that she knew better than I how to raise kids. Another mistake made. A proper bond with my children was not established because of this advice, and the fact that I was gullible enough to listen to it.

I later found myself in a panic as to how to deal with these little people. I knew how to feed them, clothe them, and after my husband and I separated, I kept a roof over their heads and taught them how to behave like "nice" little boys and girls, but when it came to actual nurturing, I didn't even know such a thing existed. I had no idea that it was up to me to let them know how important they were. I assumed they automatically knew that, and I also assumed that they knew they were loved. The ridicule of my father, and my mother's inability to fill in the gaps, had done more damage than I had realized. The emptiness that I carried inside was what I had to give, and so I passed it on.

My children also had to witness the rage that I carried. The multitude of screams that I had been unable to express through my childhood had been stuffed down for so long that the compartment that contained them had reached full capacity, and each new problem that would come up now would only add more pressure as I tried to stuff even more agony into an already-filled holding tank. I would explode. I would scream and rant and rave like a mad woman over what would seem to be the most trivial things. I had learned no coping skills, so I had no idea how to handle life.

I was almost as strict with my kids, as my father had been with me, not allowing them to go many places, because I was terrified that something would happen to either one of them, and I wouldn't know what to do. I had become, like my mother, terrified of life. I had wanted to experience life in the normal fashion, like other kids, while I was growing up, but since that had been denied, I now found myself denying the experience of a normally active life to my children because of an unidentified terror of the very thing I had always longed for.

I couldn't easily make a decision as to what would be okay for them and what wouldn't, because I assumed that any decision I made would be wrong, and then the whole world would know what my father had known...that I was an idiot. It was bad enough that I believed this, but I would become paralyzed at the thought of the entire universe laughing at my children because they had a moron for a mother. It was easier to ask them not to ask me to go out among others and have to pretend that I was as good as anyone else. That would require more acting ability than I could muster in that time of my life. I just couldn't take the chance that I would ruin it for everyone. My God, I had BECOME my parents... BOTH of them, combined! I had become the embodiment of my mother's fears and my father's rage. The one thing I didn't adopt from my father was his child-molesting tendencies, and at least I was happy about that, until I realized years later that, although I was never sexually abusive with my children, I had become a child molester in an entirely different avenue. When I read the definition of "molest", and saw that it meant to "interfere with", I realized that any time I had denied my children the right to pursue a normal, active, and creative life, due to the fears and phobias that I had developed over the years, I had actually "interfered with", or "molested" their souls, and wounded their spirits. The guilt of THAT was hard to deal with.

My father's restrictions that he had raised me in were all too evident in the way I limited my OWN children's activities. Do I blame my parents for this? I did for a long time, until I realized that they had been crippled, too, and had done the best they could from behind the bars of their OWN prison cells. Had they KNOWN better, they would have DONE better, but they DIDN'T, so they COULDN'T. That's just the way it is.

When one of the jobs that I had required traveling, that seemed to me to be the ideal situation. Someone else would stay with my kids while I'd be gone, and the someone else could make the decisions for each day. I always thought that anyone else would be better at that than I would, so, in my own distorted way, I felt that I was doing my kids a favor by not being there much. I was so convinced that I was an unwanted nuisance in other people's lives, that it never occurred to me that my children would want me, either. That was a horrible mistake, because not only did they want me, but they needed me, another thought that would never even occur to me for a long time. I had been taught that I had nothing to offer, so I thought I had nothing to offer to my children, either, other than to be the provider. If you don't feel special, you certainly can't make others feel special.

There were other people around that I gave my attention to, such as neighbors and friends, but I gave other people my full attention, because I was trying to fill that void inside of me. So why couldn't I give my kids that same kind of personal attention? I puzzled over this for a long time, but it wasn't until after I had entered into a relationship with God, that I finally got the answer. I sat down one day to ask Him why I couldn't give them the special attention that they had needed. Why had I been so hard on them...and so distant? His answer would open my eyes to something that I've seen over and over in others. I guess I would call it a common thread among those who've been made to feel badly about themselves.

If you are raised without a proper demonstration of love, although you may love your children dearly, down deep inside, it's almost impossible for you to demonstrate that love to them. You simply don't know HOW. You copy what you've learned at home. You keep the love you have for them hidden away in your heart, while you prepare them for life in a cold and uncaring world. After all, aren't they simply extensions of yourself? If you weren't worthy of being loved, then you have to assume that because they are a part of you, they will be equally rejected. In complete ignorance of what you're doing, you pass on the same discouragement that was passed on to you. You're not trying to be mean, and you don't want to hurt them, but you're subconsciously preparing them for life as you've experienced it.

You don't know why this world didn't want you, but you're afraid, because your children are yours, that the world won't want them, either. It makes you feel badly for them, because you really WANT them to be accepted, but you believe they won't be, just because they're extensions of you. You don't want them to get their hopes up that they're going to find their place in this world like anyone else. The fact that they naturally believe they fit in terrifies you, because you remember the times when you thought you were as good as anybody else, only to be ridiculed and laughed at to the point of total humiliation, and you'd like to spare them that from the world, so you feel it's your duty to make them understand now that they're just not going to be all that they hope they will be, rather than let them grow up with a false confidence that the world will tear away before they've gotten very far.

That's pretty much the sad reasoning of any parent who loves their child, but has had their own self-image destroyed. They've been made to believe that they and their offspring are of no value to others, and so they subconsciously begin the process of passing on their pain, for this is the legacy of the abused.

chapter **8**
FASTEN THOSE SEAT BELTS...
WE'RE GOING TO CRASH

I had become totally discouraged by the time I was twenty. It seemed like, no matter what I had tried to do, all I had actually DONE was moved from one prison situation to another. The only thing that had changed was the faces of the guards. The one positive thing that I had experienced from these twenty years was the birth of my two children, although I was too emotionally crippled by then to let them know how much I loved them, so I settled for providing what I could.

I had been taught that men were the undisputed authority in this world, but instead of finding acceptance with these authority figures, all I'd been so far was a scapegoat for their mockery or their rage. I had finally had enough. I shattered like a too-thin piece of glass that's been thrown around one too many times. I looked around one day and discovered that I was no longer bewildered by my life, but had become instead, just plain furious! I was tired of trying to please people who refused to be pleased. I rebelled against everyone who had worked so hard to stuff me into whatever mold suited their needs.

Propelled by the pressure of pent-up frustration, and an unbelievably strong desire to experience life, rather than punishment, I bolted out into a world that I had been taught nothing about. I had no idea where I was going, or what I would do with my life, but I didn't care, either. I was on a "high", just knowing that I was free. I looked at life as a great adventure that I would finally be able to experience now, rather than just wonder about. Naively believing that people could be trusted, save most that I'd had previous experience with, I set out to meet these wonderful creatures and finally find my place.

From the time I was young, if I had innocently said someone was nice, my mother would respond with a warning that people were NOT as nice as I thought they were, and that I'd be lucky to find three real friends in my entire lifetime. She never told me why she believed this, but would simply say it as a statement of fact, then return once again to her daily routine. I hated that statement because, in the emptiness of my childhood, I really NEEDED to believe there were good people out there. I held tightly but silently to my stubborn belief that there WERE people out there who were really worth knowing. When I finally rebelled, I set out to prove my mother wrong. She HAD to be wrong. Otherwise, what reason would I have to want to BE in this world? It took a while, and a few more wounds, before I sadly surrendered to my mother's life-long philosophy. I had set out bravely, with my band-aids on my wounds, to find those nice people I so needed to believe in. What I found instead was that wounded people, like wounded animals, hold a particularly strong magnetic appeal for the vultures in this world.

Within a couple of years, I had given up my hopeful expectations, and slipped quietly back into my survival mode. I still wanted to experience life, but by now I didn't really care if that experience was good, bad, or otherwise. At least, I figured, it was SOMETHING, as opposed to the stagnation I had learned to despise.

As hope gave way to bitterness, I continued on. I couldn't go back, for that would have meant returning to the already-known emptiness that had driven me out in the first place. I HAD to keep going, for that's what survivors DO. I now changed my attitude, however, in the same way you would change a coat. I went now from the light spring jacket of hope, to a much heavier covering called "revenge", a much more appropriate protection against the coldness I had found.

I no longer believed that a genuine love existed that could ever take the pain away. At least, that's what my wounded spirit believed. Actually, there HAD been a couple of wonderful people that I'd met along the way, who had genuinely cared about me for the brief intervals that I would allow, but since I had been programmed to believe that I, in fact, was unlovable, I wasn't able to accept that caring as anything real, or lasting, because it couldn't fill that void deep down inside of me. No amount of caring would fit comfortably with my damaged self-image, so I continued on in a downward spiral at a faster and faster pace, heading toward my own destruction. As I plummeted downward, my bitterness and sarcasm about life increased. What I had come to believe toward the end of that spiraling, was that people who still THOUGHT love existed, were living in a bubble of illusions, and were not even aware of the reality that I had been made ALL too aware of. The "love" people believed in was merely a sham.

By the time I had hit the lowest, most rebellious time in my life, I had become completely cynical. I had come to believe that these poor deluded people needed to face the truth, and it's as though I felt it my duty to burst as many of those bubbles as people foolishly brought near me. Once their illusions were shattered, I could easily walk away with a stone-cold sense of satisfaction, knowing that I had just shared a taste of what REAL life was all about. I could see no sense any longer in these people living in their silly fantasies, when I absolutely KNEW that there was no truth to the love they thought was in their lives. Having earlier tossed aside all the rules and regulations I'd been taught as though they were so many chains in a prison escape, I had slowly but surely become a devious creature that couldn't be trusted with the hearts or feelings of anyone. Fueled by revenge against a world in which I felt I had no place, I had grown to despise the ones the world had given place to. By now, disappointment and crushed hopes had created in me a stone-cold heart, with a mind to match. Nothing penetrated any more. I said before that a wounded human is like a wounded animal. They may survive, but if you get too close, they might just tear you to pieces. And that's exactly what I was…a human whose wounds had become infected with bitterness and rage, and I was more than willing to share. In twenty eight years I had become hatred smiling. Nothing more, nothing less.

chapter 9
THE PSYCHOLOGY OF THE DAMNED

I had developed my survival tactics along the way, and I HAD survived, and I was proud of that. NOBODY could get anything over on me now, because I had become wise to the fact that there was no one who could be trusted, and I had learned how to beat them all at their own game. I had finally learned how to hurt others first, before they got a chance to hurt me. I had spent too many years in a psychological war zone to think any other way. The people I REALLY felt I had to be cautious of were the ones who seemed to be sincere...the trustworthy ones. Due to the fact that I'd been done in so many times by people that I had thought I could trust, I had decided by now that the ones who appeared to be trustworthy had simply honed their acting skills to a greater degree than the more obvious jerks. If I dared get involved with someone who seemed nice, the longer they were nice to me, the crazier it made me. I had learned to expect betrayal, and the longer I had to wait for it, the more nervous I would become, until I finally couldn't take the suspense any longer, and I would have to initiate the betrayal myself. After all, betrayal WAS what was to be expected, wasn't it? Nice people just didn't fit comfortably with what my belief system had become.

Peaceful relaxation was not an option for me, for I had learned that I would have to keep my guard up if I were going to make it through another day, another year, another relationship, another ANYTHING. Keeping my guard up was tiresome, though, and sometimes I'd retreat from others and enter my solitude again, just for a time of refreshing.

During my first marriage, I'd discovered the world of books, and I would return to book reading during those times of solitude. I had found that if I couldn't find a way to break free from my emotional prison, and go out to experience life myself in any normal way, I could at least absorb into the experiences of others by reading. I read all kinds of books, always in an attempt to find out what the authors knew, that they had generously chosen to reveal within those written pages. I loved losing myself in novels, a great escape from my otherwise mundane existence. Eventually, I even ventured into a psychology book or two, to try to get a grip on what life was about.

Being a people-studier while I was growing up hadn't gotten me the answers I was looking for. Unfortunately, I could never get close enough to anyone to find out what was inside them. It was as though I had spent my earlier years in the library of humanity, unable to do anything but study the covers, merely guessing what great mystery might be hidden inside. Once I was on my own, if someone appeared to have an interesting "cover", that would be enough to cause me to enter into some type of relationship with them. Like so much book-reading, I'd stay long enough to find out what that person was all about, then I'd be gone. I hurt a lot of people when I did this, including myself, but that had never been my intention. I simply had an insatiable desire to find that missing piece in the puzzle that was my life. I just KNEW that SOMEWHERE there was SOMETHING that would fill that void inside me that kept me in a perpetual state of loneliness. I entered relationship after relationship, each time hoping to find the answer, but the answer was never there. As soon as I would realize that this was the case, I'd lay the relationship aside like a finished novel, having no desire to read it over and over again. Once it was read, it was read, and I'd move on to the next, still searching. This quest did nothing to enhance my reputation, but rather to destroy it. I wasn't concerned with that, though, despite the warnings of others. I HAD to find what I was looking for, and I was still sure that SOMEONE had the answer.

chapter 10
JUST VISITING

My mother had come to spend a weekend with us before she and my step-father would leave for Florida for the winter. She loved being with us, and it was always a welcomed experience, except for one naggy little thing that she would always manage to do before she'd leave. I'd say that our weekend visits were perfect, except for that one little "nag", then she'd leave irritated, and I'd be upset and relieved when she went out the door. She was, for the most part, a quiet, peaceful woman now, although I couldn't understand why. Her life with my dad had not been a happy one, and she had struggled for years to survive financially before and AFTER him, and now my step-father was ill. Still, she carried a peace within her. I couldn't identify with it, but I was glad for it, because it made her a very pleasant person to be around.

Well, now she had come again with hugs and kisses, and pleasant conversation, and hadn't even done the "naggy" thing at all this time, and it was great! The weekend had flown by quickly. It was already Sunday afternoon, and mom would be leaving soon, so I figured I was off the hook this time. We'd gotten smoothly through this visit, right up to the moment of bringing her suitcase down the stairs, when she hit me with "the nag" again. DARN! I was hoping we could get through ONE weekend without this.

It always started the same way. "Vicki," she would begin, "we need to talk." She would take on a very solemn tone, and I'd know what was coming. Now the laughter and lightheartedness were gone from her voice because NOW we were going to talk about GOD. She'd have that same tone that I remembered from church, when they'd start that gloom and doom message about hell and damnation. I would recognize that tone, and immediately throw my invisible walls up to protect myself. "You need to get into a church somewhere", she would begin again. Yep, this is it! BATTLE STATIONS!! Now, I usually liked this woman, but I had concluded that there must be something downright sadistic about her, because it never failed that she was going to start preaching to me. GOOD GRIEF! I HAD BEEN RAISED IN A CHURCH! You'd think the woman would REMEMBER that. She's the one who TOOK me! And I had faithfully attended , too, since I wasn't really allowed to go anywhere else. I had also realized a long time ago that there was nothing going on in that place to make me want to go back, once I'd left home. It wasn't that they weren't nice people, mind you, and very sincere in their belief, I suppose, but I had never found anything there that could even HINT at taking the sadness out of my life.

They were forever getting these preachers to come there for revival services. They'd go on about hellfire and damnation until you were afraid to leave the building, because they never forgot to warn you that you could be struck down by a disaster on the other side of those doors, and if you hadn't gotten "saved", you'd end up in the eternal fires of hell and be stuck there forever. I guess it was the people who were "saved" that always left there smiling. I'd always leave depressed. God, life wasn't swell to start with, and now I had THIS to look forward to? I didn't feel safe to start with, and I just couldn't bring myself to hand me over to a God who had left me in the quiet misery that I lived in. Why bother? It didn't seem to me that He cared much about me, either. I hadn't found life in that church building, any more than I had at home, which was the reason for my plunging into whatever mischief I could get into in the world, in the FIRST place.

This, of course, was the reason for my mother bringing this subject up every time we came face-to-face. Sure, I was screwing my life up big time, but what was the big deal now? She hadn't considered talking about any problems I might have while my life was being ruined, so I certainly had no intention of discussing my ruined life with her NOW! By now, I resented ANYONE trying to tell me what I needed, when no one had bothered to care what I needed when I had been silently screaming for help for years. And now that I'd decided to find out for myself what life was about, so WHAT if I was making a mess of it? I might not be living my life right in the eyes of others, but at least I was LIVING it. (and with a vengeance, I might add). I had broken through the bars of that childhood prison, and was running wild and free. I didn't need anyone trying to pretend that they cared NOW. I had already figured out the "concerned" people's game, anyway. They didn't want me to embarrass them . Too bad! They certainly hadn't cared about MY embarrassment all those years.

I had survived a lot of distasteful situations because I had learned how to mentally and emotionally disconnect from those situations while they were happening. I had found that if I disconnected, it was as though the distasteful situation was not happening at all. I had become an expert at this little survival technique when I was young, so by now I had no problem whatsoever disconnecting from anything that made me uncomfortable. As a matter of fact, RIGHT NOW seemed like a very good time to put this technique into action.

"You need God in your life". My mother had begun the agonizing conversation again. She took one look at my disinterested face, and quietly deflated. She could see I wasn't going to listen again, and she gave up more easily this time, much to my relief. She cut the confrontation short with "Well, Vicki, I don't know what ever will become of you, but I can see there's just no use talking to you about this any more. Maybe you're just so wrapped up in your own sin that you can't hear the truth, no matter what anyone says. Did you see where I laid my jacket?"

Once we got her belongings into the car and did the goodbye kisses and hugs, I began to relax a little. We waved goodbye as we watched her car heading down the road, and I released a long, slow sigh of relief. I wouldn't have to go through this confrontation again until she returned in the spring. With that thought, leaving the kids outside to play with their friends, I turned and headed back to my apartment, and back to the emptiness I had become accustomed to. "Maybe your just so wrapped up in your own sin that you can't hear the truth..." That phrase would return to haunt me many times in the next few weeks. Sometimes I'd wonder if it were true, but then I'd shake off that eerie feeling that would accompany that statement, and go on with my life. I worked, I laughed, I argued, I drank, I screamed, I'd go into a rage for no apparent reason, and every now and then, when the inner turmoil would peak and tears would fill my eyes, I'd learned that a sharp, deep breath and a quick shake of my head would bring back the control that I needed to get me through another day. These times of tears trying to surface were becoming more frequent now, so I had to work harder at pretending I was happy when others were around.

chapter 11
THE COLLISION

I've always viewed my spiritual awakening as a type of "head-on collision". Others, upon hearing me use this phrase, would immediately become concerned and ask how bad the accident had been, but the event that I was referring to was a different KIND of collision. I'd been moving at such a high speed of rage, that when I accidentally ran "head-on" into the person of Jesus Christ, it had an effect on me similar to hitting an invisible wall that brought me to a dead-stop. It wasn't at all a violent experience. It was just the opposite, actually, but the moment of meeting Him and knowing that He was real, made an impact on my life far greater than any car accident ever could have. I was all of a sudden totaled, but in a surprisingly refreshing way.

After I had successfully dodged my mother's latest attempt at converting me to her way of thinking, I finally confronted God in what I later came to call my first prayer. Pathetic as it was, it was me, and it was real. My most recent unfulfilling relationship had just disintegrated, and suffice it to say I was in my pit ...again. Feeling MORE than just a little sorry for myself, I finally began to spew some of my rage out at God. Bear with me on this one, because I'm sure this isn't what you've been taught that prayer usually consists of. The "prayer" went something like this...

"Okay, God, IF you even exist! I just want you to know that I DON'T WANT TO KNOW YOU! And if you DO exist, which I don't really believe anyway, I DON'T CARE!! As far as I'm concerned, IF you exist, and I think I'm talking to WALLS here, you're nothing more than a sadistic creep that sits up there on your fancy throne, watching people hurt themselves over and over again, and LAUGHING! Well I HOPE, if you DO exist, that you're having a good laugh THIS time. My mother keeps saying that I need to know you. What a joke! She doesn't even KNOW that you probably don't exist. And if you DO exist, nobody's going to tell ME that you care about ANYBODY! Her life's not so great either, you know, so she can believe whatever she WANTS to believe, but it's not for ME. I only have ONE question, though...one STINKING THING I don't understand. Why is she so PEACEFUL about it? THAT DRIVES ME NUTS! I've never understood the peace that woman has, cause I've done everything I know to have that, and it doesn't exist. Well anyway, I don't expect I'd ever get an answer to THAT one either, since I figure I'm just talking to WALLS here, but if you DO exist, I just wanted you to know that I DON'T want to know you! I almost wish I did, but there's nothing in me that's interested. I actually wish you could MAKE me interested. If you've got enough power to do THAT help YOURSELF, but like I said, there's just nothing in me that cares."

I had embellished this speech with a myriad of choice curse words that I have chosen not to share, out of mercy for the reader. With that all out of my system, I went to bed, considering that I had finally flipped further than ever before. GOOD GRIEF! I had just told off a wall!

Now, I wouldn't by any means have considered that the garbage that had just come out of my mouth that evening was a prayer any more than YOU would, but apparently God did, because He answered it. Only a couple of nights later would I find myself unable to sleep, having nothing to read, and settling for reading a religious book that my mother had very not-so-discreetly left behind on one of her weekend visits. I didn't even want to open this book, but then it dawned on me that this was the perfect solution to my dilemma. I could use this book as a sedative! What the heck! A couple of pages of this stuff would put me to sleep in no time. Imagine my surprise when this "religious" book captured my interest, and I was up half the night reading. Who would have thought it? The book was a fiction novel about the Rapture, which I had heard about all the while I was growing up.

I didn't find anything in that book that made me want to go to church, but what I DID find was a character in the book who had seen something, toward the end of the story, that was powerful enough to die for. Now I was impressed. I'd been raised around Christians, but I'd never seen anything like that. It seemed to me that what I had witnessed so far was people who believed in God, but no one who ever talked about anything powerful enough to make any significant difference. They all just seemed to be people with more problems than most people, and that wasn't too appealing to someone like me. I needed ANSWERS, not just some blind faith that would somehow get me through this life, but leave me still feeling like I wasn't worth anything. Now a new question haunted me. What had she SEEN? I wanted to know. I read the book again, which created even more curiosity as to what had happened to that girl. I needed to know what she had SEEN.

A few nights later, I found myself in the same predicament... no sleep, and nothing new to read. I began searching the house like an addict looking for a fix. How was I going to make it through this evening with nothing to take my mind off my circumstances? Disgusted, I muttered a few curses, then finished with "My God! Isn't there ANYTHING left in this house that I haven't already read?" At that moment, a memory from the past flashed across my mind.

There had been a little blue book, I recalled, that had traveled with me for about five years, when my job had called for traveling, It was always in the inside pocket of my suitcase. I never knew how the book had made it's way into that suitcase, but I'd never paid enough attention to it to even bother to throw it out. It had been given to me about ten years earlier by a religious group, which explained why I'd never opened it, and now here I was, desperate for something to read, and wondering if it could still be in there. I hadn't even used that suitcase for the last two or three years, but now I dragged it out of the back of my closet, plopped it onto my bed, and unzipped it. I slipped my hand down inside that pocket, and there was that little book, after all these years. I didn't care WHY it was still there, I was just glad that it was.

That little blue book had traveled with me for so long, unread, that I now removed it from it's pocket gently, as though it were an old friend that I hadn't seen in a long time. It had survived this long because it had been hidden. So had I. I figured this little book and I had something in common. It was time to see what was in it. I put the suitcase away, and laid across my bed with that little book, happy to have found a distraction for the night.

I had only read the first couple of pages, when I sensed a strangely different feeling that had come over the room. My attention was drawn upward, away from the book, as though by a powerfully magnetic presence. My eyes widened and my jaw dropped in awe as I found myself staring at two figures standing by my bed. I immediately knew that one of them was Jesus, and standing beside Him, I instinctively knew, was His Father. There they were, and I had the most powerful impression that they were discussing something. They were not physical men, for although everything in me was totally aware of them, I knew they were far beyond flesh and blood. It was as though I was looking into a different realm that had just opened up in my room.

As I stared, wide-eyed, all I could think was "You're REAL! Oh, my God, you're REAL! I didn't know you were REAL!" I was right this moment in the very presence of what I'd been searching for, for twenty eight years. I had never before even DREAMED that such an overwhelming sense of love could exist. It was powerful in it's gentleness. It was drawing, and it was satisfying. It was magnetic, and it was awesome! It was so beautiful, that it was overwhelming. There was something eternal in that moment of awakening, and for the time of that connection, no more than a minute, I was aware of nothing, other than the deepest love I had ever longed for. I was in the presence of Love Itself, in all of it's purity. And I knew now that They had ALWAYS loved.

I began to cry. I kept whispering over and over "I'm so sorry. I didn't KNOW that you loved people. I'm so sorry. If I'd known you loved people, I wouldn't have lived my life like this. I didn't KNOW …I didn't KNOW. My God, you actually CARE about people! I'm so sorry…I'm so, so sorry. I never knew you loved me. I didn't know anybody did. I really need You in my life. If You can fix my life, please do…please." With that, I surrendered to a world of sobs. I don't know how long I cried, but I know I fell asleep that way.

When I awoke in the morning, there was no evidence of what had happened in that room the night before, other than a tear-stained page on the opened book that had been my pillow for the night.

chapter 12

THE MORNING AFTER

I laid the book aside as I got up to begin the day, giving no more than a momentary thought to what had happened the night before. I couldn't. One glance at the clock jarred me away from any further retrospection, while I moved quickly into the routine of waking children for school, and heading downstairs to get their breakfast ready. This day was starting out the same as any other, I thought, until I came down the stairs to find the sun pouring through the living room windows. I was so startled by that sunshine, as though I'd never EVER seen it before, that I stopped in the middle of the room and just stood there for a minute, completely in awe of the beauty of it. Now why, I wondered, had I never noticed that before? I shook my head and walked into the kitchen.

As I was preparing breakfast, I began to notice something else that was just a little puzzling. Everything around me seemed lighter somehow. This was odd, I thought, and every now and then, during breakfast, I would glance around the room, sort of "checking the atmosphere", and each time I got the same impression...yep, it felt LIGHTER, in somewhat the same way that air feels lighter after a nearly-unbearable pressure of humidity has been lifted by a summer storm. By the time the kids had darted out the door to go to the school bus, I had become aware of something even MORE subtle going on in ME. In awe again, I realized that the heaviness of the inner pain that I had always carried, was missing. I wasn't feeling angry, or scared, or guilty, or confused, or pressured, or depressed, or embarrassed, or hopeless, and those were things that were ALWAYS with me. It was as though all the years of all the pain and all the turmoil had somehow vanished! Everything inside me felt gently and quietly still. This, I thought, must be what peace feels like.

The night of my awakening to the reality of Jesus and His Father had caused much more to take place in me than I could comprehend. Within a couple of days, I found myself being curiously drawn to another book that my mother had deposited with me on one of her earlier visits. It was a copy of the Living Bible that she had given me a couple of years earlier, disguised as a birthday gift, in yet another failed attempt at changing my life. Until now it had graced my coffee table as a sign of respect for her when she came to visit, but I had never until now even CONSIDERED it as reading material. NOW, however, this book seemed to possess the same invisible drawing power that an off-limits cookie jar emits to a four-year old. I couldn't resist the temptation to see what was in it. A new fascination began to take hold of me the day I opened that book and began to read. Instead of finding the gloom and doom that I had always thought was in there, due to my childhood church experience, I found instead that this book was a combination of beautiful, logical, and even humorous, statements of truth. I was reading Proverbs. I had read a lot of books, but never anything so intriguing as this one. The more I read, the more I wanted to read. I would get my kids off to school each morning, straighten the house, and reward myself with hours of devouring the very book that had been so repulsive to me before. Most days would find me still reading when the kids got home from school.

As much as I loved reading this Bible, after a few weeks I began to wish I had someone to read WITH. I was so enjoying this experience of truth that it just seemed natural to me to have someone to share it with. No sooner had the wish become noticeable to me, than I had the opportunity to offer a neighbor a ride to a doctor's appointment that she would otherwise have had to cancel. I had never spoken with this lady before, other than an acknowledging "Hi" if we happened to pass on the sidewalk, but another neighbor had mentioned this lady's transportation dilemma, and I had easily responded. It all seemed simple enough. She needed a ride...I had a car...how hard is that to put together? I had sent the neighbor back to the lady with the message that I would be happy to take her. I was about to learn how valuable it can be to meet someone else's need.

Apparently, a wish really IS like a prayer, because this quiet, gentle woman knocked on my door a few minutes before we were to leave, and I invited her in. She took one look at my Bible laying open on the kitchen table, and looked at me in surprise, asking if I was reading that. When I explained that I had just recently begun, I asked if SHE had ever read the Bible. She responded with a shy smile, and said that she had read her Bible almost daily for nearly seventeen years, but had always wanted someone to read with her. WOW! Could this get any better?

I responded again, this time with an excitement I could hardly contain. We made our plan that day to get children off to school the following day, do our morning chores, then meet in my apartment for coffee and reading. The day after THAT, we met in HER apartment. We zig-zagged back and forth between her house and mine every weekday for months like this, reading, one chapter at a time, for hours a day, and discussing what we saw in each chapter. We were like two happy school children, anxiously awaiting each new day and each new lesson. What I had initially assumed would be a trip together to a singular doctor's appointment, ended up blossoming into a multitude of visits together to study The Great Physician.

I hadn't said anything to anyone about my spiritually awakening experience, even when people who knew me would stop me on the sidewalk or in the grocery store and ask me what was different about me. When I'd say "Nothing", they would insist that yes, something was definitely different. I would watch their eyes dart from my face to my hair, then to my clothes, trying to identify this difference, but since they could only perceive the OUTSIDE of me, they would walk away still wondering, and I'd walk away smiling, and holding this awareness of Jesus close to my heart. I didn't even tell the lady I shared Bible reading with. I didn't keep that experience to myself because I was embarrassed about it, but I kept it hidden because I was so in AWE of it. I had met someone so precious in the person of Jesus Christ, and had fallen

so DEEPLY in love with Him, that I considered this event too special to expose to what I still considered to be a very sadistic world.

I've heard people, even ministers, over the years talk about
their own surrender to God as though they were instantly
changed into perfection, and I've wondered if that were true.
I don't question other people's experience though, for that is
THEIR experience, but for me, that simply was not the case. I had
been so wrecked by the time the Lord changed my direction, that
although I was now starting out on a new road, it didn't change
the fact that I was in dire need of repair, and a lot of it.

chapter 13
OFF TO CHURCH WE GO!

Soon I began to entertain the idea of going to church. Yep, a heck of a good idea! I was READY to start taking my kids to church. I expressed this intention to a couple of my neighbors and found a strange thing happening each time I mentioned it. I would no sooner say I wanted to find a church to go to, when the word " Baptist" would flash in front of my face like a neon sign coming on, then it would be gone. I couldn't imagine why this happened, so I would dismiss it as soon as it would flash. I had no intention of attending a Baptist church. It wasn't that I had anything against Baptist, I simply had an idea of my own. I wanted to find a church like my mother and I had attended for a brief time with my aunt when I was eleven years old. All I could remember was that it was called a "spirit-filled" church, and although I didn't really know what that meant at the time, I never forgot what it felt like in that cozy little place. The people there were mostly poor like myself, I had guessed from the way they dressed, but there was a warm, friendly feeling in that place that was different from the church I had been used to. I remembered my mother and my aunt talking about speaking in tongues, and I knew they did this there, but I was eleven, and more interested in talking to the minister's daughter, who was my age, and had become my temporary friend. At that time, the "God stuff" was left to the adults.

So, I finally set about finding a church. I looked in the phone book under churches, when I came across "Pentecostal Churches." Not only had I heard about Pentecost on the TV show that we watched, and read about it in my Bible, but I remembered hearing about it in that little church from years ago. This would work. This was where we needed to go. Again, the word "Baptist" flashed. I dismissed this intrusion into my thoughts as quickly as it came. I had found us a church, and it was only five minutes away, in the next little town north of us. I knew I'd have no trouble locating the church in this little town, for they only had a few streets. How hard could it be?

Our clothes were ready, tomorrow was Sunday, and the alarm clock was set. The next morning was fun for all three of us, getting ready to go. My kids hadn't attended church since my mother had taken them, and twelve years had passed since I'd been inside a church building. One final inspection, and we were ready. I drove up to that little town and drove around and around. Then I drove around and around again. I couldn't seem to find this little church anywhere, which made no sense at all. Where could they possibly have hidden it in this little place? I'd already gone up and down every street they had, TWICE, and hadn't even seen anyone on the street to ask. This was too weird. I kept watching the time... it was getting later and later. I knew by now we were missing the Sunday School time.

"What am I going to do now!" I breathed the question, never expecting an answer. "Baptist" flashed again, and I slumped. I felt defeated now. I hadn't intended to go to a Baptist church, but I couldn't FIND the other one. "Oh, God," I groaned, and it was as though an invisible voice laughed softly and said, "NOW are you ready to go to the Baptist?"

"Yes", I sighed, "let's go find a Baptist."

Since I'd already toured this little town thoroughly, I knew there was no Baptist Church there, so we drove back to our own town to see what we could find. Once we got there, I saw a man I knew walking down Main Street. As a matter of fact, he was the one I'd broken up with before I'd met the Lord, and I hadn't seen him in weeks. Of course, he was heading to a club that was open on Sunday mornings. I pulled my car over to the curb just ahead of where he was walking, and he strolled over to my car, a big smile on his face. I asked him if there was a Baptist Church in town, and he looked as though his eyes were going to pop out of his head as he exclaimed, "You're looking for a CHURCH?"

"Yes," I answered impatiently, "do you know if there's a Baptist Church in town?"

Pushing aside his obvious shock, he managed to say, "Make a left at the corner, and go up a couple of blocks. It's a brick building on the right...at least I THINK that's a Baptist Church."

"Thanks," I said hurriedly, and started pulling out from the curb. As I made that left, I glanced back to see him still standing there, watching us go up the hill as though he couldn't believe what he was seeing. He had only seen me in bars before, and he had known me well enough to be shocked that I was looking for a church. We had missed Sunday School because of the driving time, but we made it into the building before the church service began. It wasn't an unpleasant experience, so we went again the following Sunday, on TIME this time, and thus, my children and I began our separate Sunday School classes, then church together.

It wasn't long after that that Tony, the man who had given me the directions to the church that Sunday, re-entered my life. We had had such a stormy relationship before that I wasn't too sure about starting this up again. Common sense said we had no business being together. Tony believed otherwise. My son, now twelve years old, wasn't going to tolerate another round of this insanity, and had made up his mind to go live with his dad. This ripped my heart out, but I also understood why he needed his dad so badly. Even though God was now a part of my life, I was like anyone else who's really messed up and has to start over. As much as I wanted to fight against him leaving, in my heart I knew that I had failed miserably, and I was glad he was now free to have a better life. No matter how devastated I was over his leaving, I at least knew that he would be safe with his dad. I reverted back to my old survival tactic when my son left. I became numb inside, and detached myself from the thought that he was gone. This was pain I couldn't deal with, and wouldn't be able to for a long, long time.

Tony and I ended up getting married not too long after that, and moved into an old house that had been his family's "homestead". My daughter and I continued to go to the Baptist Church, but I no longer lived close enough to the lady who had become my Bible partner, and my friend, to conveniently continue our study together. I continued my daily Bible studying on my own.

Then a Sunday morning came when my attention became riveted to a lady who was already sitting in the church when we arrived. I hadn't seen her there before, but now I couldn't help but notice this woman who appeared to be absorbed in prayer, while everyone else wandered around visiting. Her head was bowed, and although she wasn't making a sound, her lips were moving slightly, and she appeared to be oblivious to everything that was going on around her. Then, as I continued to watch, discreetly of course, she stopped praying and seemed now to be quietly listening to something. The look on her face was radiant, unlike the others, and I knew that this woman had a relationship with the Lord that was far more meaningful than anything I had seen before. Everything in me wanted to know this lady, for although I wasn't sure what it was exactly that made her different from the rest, there was definitely a difference, and I needed to know what she had that the others didn't.

The following Sunday morning she was there again when we arrived. Again she was deeply in prayer, while others socialized. I sat a couple of rows behind her, and wished again that I could meet this woman who was so serious about the reason she was in this building. I sat there watching her, curious about her, when all of a sudden she turned around, looked straight into my eyes, and said "Good morning. Are you sitting by yourself?" I was so startled by this, that I nearly stuttered when I answered that yes, I was, and she immediately responded with " Oh, Honey, come sit with me. It's no fun sitting by yourself." I breathed an astonished "Thank You, Lord!" and quietly moved forward a couple of rows.

We exchanged names and chatted briefly, then at the end of the service, she asked if I were involved in a Bible study anywhere. When I told her I wasn't, she invited me to a weekly Bible study in the home of another lady in town. It was a Tuesday morning Bible study, she said, with just a few people getting together. I had never heard of people having group Bible study in their homes, but I was more than happy to join them. What an adventure this was turning out to be. By now I was glad the word "Baptist" had kept flashing, and that I hadn't been able to find the other church. I was finally starting to get the point that the word "Baptist" that had kept invading my mind was actually one of God's ways of communicating His direction for me. He had been putting a sign post in front of me, and I had tried to go another way. I've come to realize since, that He was directing me to where He knew He could connect me with someone who would play a vital role in my learning experience.

By the way, there was a time later when I went back to that other town where I had looked for the church I couldn't find. This time it wasn't hidden at all. Actually it was easy to find. As it turned out, it had always been there. Go figure!

chapter 14
WHERE'S THE CLOSET...
I NEED TO CHANGE

That first in-home Bible study that I attended with my new found friend would certainly not be my last, despite the fact that I had left there the first day embarrassed. I wasn't embarrassed because of anything that had happened, but rather because of what had not. The ladies that I met that morning were relaxed, friendly, and welcoming, which put me at ease right away. After a time of reading and prayer together, the lady who had invited me turned to me and asked if I'd been baptized in the Spirit. I knew what she was talking about. I'd been faithfully watching a TV ministry since I'd met the Lord and they often referred to this baptism, and all that it entailed. I had already read all of the Scriptures that talked about it, and since I had wanted ALL that God has to offer to His kids, I'd asked God for this gift for nearly two years with no result.

I had recently given up on asking, concluding that this must not be part of God's plan for me. It was a little disappointing to not receive what I knew others HAD, but I didn't question it, either. I had become accustomed to hearing "no" concerning my requests from the time I was young, so I had learned to readily accept silence as my "no". Asking "why" had brought punishment when I was growing up, so I no longer bothered wasting time with "whys" when it came to having requests denied. I had spent years watching others receive things that I could not, so I was by now quite comfortable with being the one who stood on the sidelines, watching. It wasn't a big pity party, it was just an accepted way of life.

I explained to the lady that I didn't think that I was meant to have that, and was curiously startled when she responded with laughter. It wasn't a harsh or mocking laugh, but rather a gently amused laugh, as though this wasn't the first time she'd heard THIS story. She explained to me that God gives the gift of the Holy Spirit to ALL of His children, not just some, and asked if I would like prayer for this. She had displayed such confidence when she talked about God giving to ALL of His children, that her confidence resurrected my faith in receiving something that everyone else in the room already had. Maybe this WAS for me! I readily agreed to the prayer.

She placed her hand on my forehead, and began to pray. The others joined in that prayer in agreement with her, and nothing happened. Soon I began to inwardly cringe in embarrassment, not so much because nothing was happening, but more because I had opened myself up to being denied in front of other people again. God, how I wished I'd never even thought that I could have this. I appeared calm on the outside, but inside I was a little girl again, experiencing the same shame and frustration that any child experiences when "request denied" has been repeatedly stamped upon their souls. I left there that day smiling and exchanging hugs with everyone, letting them know that I was looking forward to the meeting next week. I HAD enjoyed the morning, and I was more than grateful that no one mentioned that prayer again. I walked out of that house that day determined to come back, and equally determined to never ask for the Baptism in the Spirit again.

There's something powerful about people praying together in agreement, whether you think there's power there or not. I had assumed that the prayer for me had failed, so I had abandoned all faith in it immediately. I would soon discover that it was THEIR faith, not mine, that would enable God to break through my hidden barriers.

A few days later, I was busy vacuuming the living room when a word was impressed on my mind. I probably wouldn't have paid it much attention, but it remained there, gently lodged in the front of my mind like an implant. The word was Shiloh. I was aware of it for a while before a startling thought occurred to me. What if this was the beginning word of the prayer language that accompanies the Baptism in the Spirit? Oh, my! Now THAT thought got my attention a lot quicker than the word itself had.

I became momentarily excited about this word, until I realized that this was not an unknown language at all, but rather a word that I was already familiar with. I even knew of a ministry by that name. As quickly as I had gotten excited about the word, the excitement subsided and I went back to my work. The word stayed with me though, and soon another thought occurred to me. Shiloh was not a word that I used in MY everyday conversation. What if…what if…what if…? I had heard a minister's wife say once that she had only ever received ONE WORD in an unknown language when she had been baptized in the Holy Spirit. She had encouraged everyone to use whatever they were given, even if it was just one word, for she said that one word spoken, that is given by the Holy Spirit, is more powerful than using a whole language that we've already learned, for it is the Spirit of GOD now speaking. I didn't think this was the case with this word, but what if it WAS, and why was it here?

Out of sheer curiosity, I continued to run the sweeper, while I kept repeating "Shiloh…Shiloh…Shiloh", and it soon began to change in the pronunciation. It was now becoming more like "Sheelah…Sheelah…Sheelah." As I continued on, now repeating this new pronunciation, it changed ever-so-slightly again. Now what I was hearing was Eshilah...Eshilah…Eshilah. I was amazed at this turn of events with this word, and even more curious now to see what would happen with it as I kept repeating it. I was so enjoying the beautiful sound of the word, that I probably would have repeated it anyway, just to listen to it. I finished the day with the word, with no further changes.

The following morning found me anxious to return to this repetitive procedure, and that day another word was added. I repeated both words the rest of the day, when I could. Each day I continued on, and each day an additional word was added, until I knew that I was no longer repeating just words, but I was making a complete statement, over and over. The more I verbalized it, the firmer it became, until my statement had become a declaration.

The forming of this declaration had taken place over a period of five days. I had no idea what it meant, but I didn't care, either. Just listening to these words rolling off my tongue held a satisfaction of it's own.

I'd been under the impression that since I'd met the Lord, I'd become complete and whole. What had always been missing from my life had finally arrived, and I felt loved. However, I had been such a mess at the time of meeting Him, that I didn't realize that meeting Him was just the beginning. I thought it was the end. I was soon going to run right into a new revelation. This conversion experience had completely changed me from being a total mess into now being a totally "saved" mess. Who knew? I certainly didn't. I'd been doing so much better now. I had entered into my second marriage now, and I was going to church now...life was reasonable these days. And now I had this new development. Except for the absence of my son, my life couldn't be better, or so I thought, until the Lord decided to show me otherwise.

My husband's ex-wife would drop their son off on Friday afternoons, then pick him up again on Sunday evenings. He was in grade school at the time, and one Sunday night she was particularly late coming to get him, so I had him get ready for bed at our house. Soon he was sound asleep and still she hadn't come, so I figured he'd be going home in the morning to get ready for school. Much later, after we'd all been asleep for the night, I was awakened by the sound of a car that had been left running in the middle of the street, in front of our house. I got up to see what was going on. I answered a knock on the door to find my husband's ex-wife standing there, asking for her son.

What nerve, I thought, to come here this late at night and ask me to drag this child out of a sound sleep. Like a pinball machine who's just had a series of balls thrust into action, I spewed out judgment after judgment against her. No sooner would an angry thought hit my mind, than it would bounce off, plunge into to my throat, and be hurled out of my mouth at a rapid-fire speed. I was good at this game. I'd had years of practice. When all the balls had been fired, the game was over, and I firmly shut the door.

My husband had been awakened when I had gotten up, and he had entered the kitchen just in time to witness my point-blank opinion, and as I marched indignantly out of the room, I could hear him re-opening the door, and asking his ex-wife to wait a minute, telling her that he'd get the boy ready. I listened to the peaceful sounds of him waking his son, getting him dressed, and sending him off with his mother, and the contrast between his peaceful behavior right then, versus my thundering just moments ago, was like a sharp slap right across my ego, forcing me to wake up to a reality I didn't want to see.

I was now humiliated with the way I had behaved. I was the one who should have been the peaceful one, not him, but instead I had become a self-righteous creep! What was it that had taken me over? Complete rage? Absolutely! Why? What was the big deal with me, anyway?

Although I now operated under a different set of standards than I used to, because of what I was learning with God, who was I to judge something that someone else did that was not nearly as bad as things that I had done before, in all the rebellion that I had lived in? What I had just done to this woman was completely unacceptable for a child of God, and I knew it. I was horrified as I realized that I had just shown someone who didn't know the Lord, just how rotten a "Christian" could really be. I had blown it, and I knew it. Everything that had rushed up out of my innermost being had said I had the right to feel that I was better than her...even more caring than her when it came to her own son. Who had I thought I was, and why hadn't I been able to stop this ridiculous outburst?

I came to find out, before the night was over, that it was nothing more than self- righteousness that had kicked in to wound another human being. Self-righteousness, not God, had raised up to screech that I was better than a lady who hadn't even met Him yet.

I had wanted so badly to be an example of how God's love could change people, and now what I had displayed was just the opposite. I hadn't changed at all. I was shattered. I burst into quiet sobs at the thought of how horribly I had acted. I had thought that I was doing so well, only to find out that I was still able to be the monster I had been before. The worst, and most devastating thought I had to deal with now, was the thought that this woman would never want to know God EVER, and it was all because of ME!

While I stammered out these things to God, amidst the torrent of tears that flowed, I begged Him to forgive me, convinced now that I had been so despicable that He'd never be able to. I just knew that I had shamed the Lord, the only one who ever truly loved me, and this was more than I could bear. My heart was broken to think that I had become an embarrassment to Him.

Then, amidst that flood of tear-dampened words, I recalled a Scripture that said that whatever comes out of our mouths, is really coming out of our hearts, and I sobbed even harder, as an even worse horror began to take shape in my mind. "Please don't leave me, Lord, PLEASE DON'T LEAVE ME!" was all that I could say now in my panic-stricken state. I knew that if He left me now, I'd never be rid of the blackness in my heart that had caused this behavior in the first place. I knew that He was the only one who could clean out my heart and make me acceptable, and I told Him so.

That night I gave up my hold on everything. I told Him to take the house, the marriage, my clothes, and even my children, and give them to someone who was fit to have any of them, for I knew now that it wasn't me. My own self-righteousness had been shown to me and now I understood why the Bible says that our righteousness is as filthy rags. I had seen what was still in me, and I was ashamed.

In the midst of this torrent, I had covered my face with a pillow from the sofa to muffle the sobs as they became deeper and harder. I was in a vice-grip of pain inside, and it seemed that nothing would ever comfort me again. "Take it all, Lord, but PLEASE DON'T LEAVE ME!", I pleaded over and over, doubting that He would ever look at me again, and desperately needing His help. A while later, another Scripture came to mind. It was the one in Romans 8 that says that all things work together for good, and the recollection of these words was like a drop of water in a dry and dusty desert. Could there be a ray of hope in this awful place?

My words to God were prayer, and that prayer went on and on, until it became so deep that I nearly became lost in it. After a while, in total emptiness and exhaustion, I realized that I was still praying, but from so deep within, that I was merely mouthing words now, but no sound was coming out of my mouth. I determined to add my voice to my prayer to find out what I was saying. To my surprise, when I applied my voice, I discovered a completely new language coming out of my mouth, one that I had never heard before, and this language was flowing fluently! Suddenly, the shame and pain that had driven me to the depths of despair seemed to evaporate as I became caught up in the joy and wonder of this beautiful language. Astonished, I now knew that God had not only NOT turned AWAY from me, but He had just given me the proof that I truly WAS His child, for He only gives that gift to His very own. This new Spirit prayer flowed on and on throughout the night. I found that I could start or stop it at will, but I chose to keep it going, just listening, amazed and grateful.

God had used the situation that night to show me my need for deeper change. Now, without the mask of my self-righteous attitude, it was easy to see I had a long way to go. I had confessed my need for change with my whole heart, nothing barred. I brokenheartedly brought the mess that I still was to Him, and he gave me instead, the power that I'd need to make those changes. That was the night I entered into God's supernatural changing room for the first time. That was the night I entered the "Prayer Closet," and once I entered, I rarely came out.

I stayed in prayer daily, for hours at a time, and I must admit that I didn't pray all the time out of a dedication to prayer, so much as I stayed there because I loved listening to it! I started to understand what the Bible meant where it said to "pray without ceasing," (I Thess.5, KJV). I had always wondered how a person could possibly DO that, but now I found myself not only ABLE to do that, but enticed to do so. Housework took on a whole new meaning for me as I went through my daily routine, listening to the most beautiful language I'd ever been privileged to hear, and it was coming out of ME!

chapter 15
LORD, I NEED A PARTNER

I had become lonely being married to a man who didn't know the Lord, and whose family wasn't showing any interest in anything spiritual. I had entertained my insatiable appetite for truth by daily Bible reading and a bevy of Christian books, but eventually I became aware of a longing inside to have someone to talk to, on a regular basis, about the Lord. I continued on in my usual routine, attending church meetings where the Bible was taught, but no one there except the minister ever talked about the Lord as though they knew Him. I kept knowing that I needed someone to talk to who really loved the Lord, but I didn't ask God for help in this area until the longing had become hard to deal with. When I did ask Him to give me someone to talk to, I was surprised by the way He met my request.

My husband's brother stopped at the house often to see my husband. His wife never came with him, but that didn't surprise me, for I knew that she was a close friend of my husband's ex-wife. One evening Tony said that he had insisted that his brother bring his wife with him the next time he came. I wanted to know why. He said that it wasn't right that we didn't know each other, since his brother was around so much. I argued this point, of course, saying that she didn't have to get to know me since she was his ex-wife's close friend, and that she'd probably not want to come to our house out of a sense of loyalty to her friend. I was satisfied with my argument, but my husband wasn't. He kept insisting, and before long, we were paid a visit by my brother-in-law and his wife, Joyce. We all sat around the kitchen table talking. Actually, the men did most of the talking, while my sister-in-law and I listened.

My sister-in-law was polite, but seemed every bit as uncomfortable as I was.

Our TV had been acting up at the time, so that evening my husband and his brother ended up in the living room working on the TV, leaving me to entertain this stranger. It might not have been so bad, if the men had stayed at the table and kept the conversation going, but when they moved to the other room I knew I was in trouble. I didn't really know this woman, so I didn't know what her interests were, to start with. I didn't know what kind of subject to pick to talk about that she wouldn't run back to her friend to tear apart. To say the least, I was not trusting THIS. Subjects would pop into my mind to talk about, but I was so nervous about the woman, I kept abandoning ideas as fast as they would come. I finally realized that there was nothing personal I was going to offer to this woman in conversation, so I figured I'd just bring up something about God. She didn't seem extremely happy at this point to be here anyway, so what did I have to lose? I figured that if she were going to criticize me, she may as well go all the way!

I began telling her about a man's testimony on a TV show about a miraculous healing he had witnessed, and instead of her giving me the polite "I can't wait to get out of here" look, she started listening intently to what I was saying, as though she had become suddenly captivated by my words. Then she told me that she had been feeling lately that there must be more to life, and that she had begun getting books from the library on spiritual subjects. Whoa! This was interesting! It turned out she was quite the book reader. She could easily read a book a day, so she frequented the library. I invited her to check out the books I had in another room, and told her that I'd be more than happy to lend her anything she'd like to read. Actually, by now I had over a couple hundred books in that room, so we went to the other room to see what might interest her.

Joyce walked out of my house that evening with an armload of books to read, and was back a week later for more. I continued to lend her books for as long as my supply lasted, then I had to appeal to friends for more. This went on for nearly a year, until she was satisfied that there really was a greater plan, and invited Jesus into her life. This was our beginning.

She and I became closer and closer as time went on. We talked about the Lord, what the Bible has to say, Christian books that we would read, and we prayed together daily. The day the power of God was released in her, and she began praying in her own prayer language, we began to go deeper into prayer. A friendship was developing between us that would form an unbreakable bond.

We attended separate churches, but remained faithful to our union. We spent time together daily in prayer, as we dealt with current problems, and finally we began to look into old wounds, take them to God, and let go of them, as He revealed these things to us. We would get together simply to see what God wanted to show us for each day. We left it up to Him to lead us. We listened to what He had to say, and questioned what He meant by His statements, and waited for Him to explain. We attended Full Gospel meetings together. We grew together in understanding.

Joyce and I have remained together as prayer partners to this day. We have both undergone much inner healing because of the time spent in prayer. I know that I never would have gotten as far as I did without my partner. I would fall into a pit of confusion, and she'd be there to pull me out. She sometimes fell into her own pit, only to need me to go to bat for her. Together we learned. We walked together, leaning on one another for strength as we hobbled down this path toward healing. We didn't criticize one another. We listened, and we prayed. If I had a bad day, I could vent with her, and visa versa, but we never left it there. Once the negative energy was released, we inevitably ended up with God to find a better way to go. After twenty-five years of prayer partnership, we still get together at least once a week to pray together, sometimes more.

People need God-appointed prayer partners. Two in agreement is a powerful thing. We need someone who will go to God on our behalf when we're down, and unable to cope. We need someone we can trust to tell anything to, someone who can listen, then go to God with us in prayer, thus getting to the heart of every problem. On days when I was too stressed to be able to hear from God, she was my ears. When she was confused and couldn't see what it was that she needed, I was her eyes. We counseled together. We went on like this for years, learning and growing, moving steadily on into the deeper things of God. She had the courage to go in whatever direction the Lord led her, and myself, I was too adventurous to tell Him no. If we didn't understand something, we took it to God together, and both became enlightened as He would reveal His knowledge. If we thought we DID understand something, we took it to God in prayer anyway, and found out more.

I'd sometimes get confused as to why some situations didn't seem to get better, because I was, after all, doing what I'd been taught in church, which was "standing on the written word of God", and the testimony of what others had been told to do in similar situations. When I asked the Lord about this, He told me that the only absolute word I would stand on was His spoken word to ME. If I applied what He had said to someone else, although it worked for them, it wouldn't necessarily work for me because He wasn't going to move on my behalf on "borrowed" instructions. If He spoke it to them, it was for them. If He spoke it to me, it was for me, and I could count on it. THAT was a major learning experience.

God goes much further in relationship with us than we know about in the beginning. He wants a one-on-one relationship with each one of us. I loved the Bible. It was my manual for life. But there's more to the relationship with God than just living "by the book". There's an intimate relationship we can have with Him that goes into much more specific instructions for each individual life, and we can have that if we take the time to be alone with Him and allow Him to equip us with the power to break through the barriers of our own minds, to get to His.

I have thanked God for years for the prayer partner He sent me. Had it been left up to me, I probably would never have even met the woman, let alone have her become my best friend. She and I have seen one another through countless healings and heartaches, and I know the reason for this is because of her dedication to the Lord, once she realized He was real. Her hunger for God matched mine. She wanted everything God had to offer, and so did I. I would think back to my past, when I was at my all-time worst and how others would ask me to attend church functions with them. I would refuse, explaining that when and IF I ever decided to go to church, I would have to go all the way with it, and I wasn't ready for that yet. I guess I always knew there was an all-the-way to go.

I'd seen too many people playing church, but very few who had ever had a real excitement about knowing the Lord. I wanted no part of that. I guess I'm just an all-or-nothing kind of person. The beauty of God's choice for my prayer partner was that she was an all-or-nothing kind of person, too. With a prayer partner, there must be total honesty. We didn't sugar-coat anything with each other. Whatever God said, we shared. We've learned not to add what we THINK He means when He speaks. We go after more information, until we understand. On occasion, we've had our misunderstandings. That's natural…we're humans, but we learned early on to address any misunderstanding or negative thought immediately, get it straightened out, and move on. Maintaining a prayer partnership is much like maintaining a marriage relationship. Being unequally yoked won't make for a successful relationship in either arena. You need a prayer partner who is sold out to God, the same as you. You and your prayer partner enter into a committed relationship, and you both must be willing to "go the distance".

A solid prayer partnership is a dangerous thing to the enemy of your soul. There's nothing more frightening to Hell Itself than two people in agreement, wholeheartedly seeking God, and all that He knows. Healing and freedom are discovered in this kind of partnership. Hell doesn't want you healed, any more than it wants you free. Hell knows that once you're free, you can set others free. NOW you've become a strong force against the very hell that once held you captive.

chapter 16
DON'T RESCUE
ME...TEACH ME!

One of the greatest things God did for me during this time of growth, was to NOT rescue me from my own mistakes, or what I CONSIDERED to be my mistakes. I had always seemed to be powerless over my own life decisions, especially concerning the affairs of the heart. I had known some wonderful men in my life, but when it came to marriage partners, I wasn't doing so well. I was now married to a second alcoholic, and living a frustrated life again because of it. My second husband, an equally wounded individual, was going to end up being one of God's greatest motivational tools in my life, but for years I just thought he'd become my greatest enemy. His violent behavior would drive me to God, over and over, begging for answers.

The day came when I finally hurled myself across my bed, crying "Why, Lord, why?" I'd had enough of this kind of misery, but I had also figured out that there had to be something drastically wrong with me that wouldn't allow me to stay with anyone who treated me well for any length of time. I needed to know why I would run from nice guys as if they had a plague, but just let me find a raging alcoholic, and I was hopelessly in love, "hopelessly" being the key word here. What the heck, I asked the Lord, was wrong with me? This had never made sense to anyone else, and it certainly didn't make sense to me.

Within days after my outburst to God about this dilemma, I had occasion to be in a Christian bookstore in a neighboring town. I had stopped in to pick up a book that had been ordered by a friend. A lady disappeared into another room to retrieve the order, and I spent that time looking around, absorbing as many book titles as I could while she was gone. A book written about getting people sober caught my attention. I was instantly outraged when I saw it. Who were they trying to kid? I knew by now that you couldn't get someone else sober if they didn't want to be. I tried to ignore the book.

I continued to browse, only to find my eyes continuously drawn back to the book about sobriety. Each time I was drawn to it, I'd become angry inside again, wondering how anyone had the NERVE to try to make people think that they could have any power over someone else's drinking habits! As the lady returned with the order, I quickly grabbed the book with the annoying title, giving in to the drawing that had become by now an irresistible force. I bought that little paperback book that day, along with the one for my friend, and left the store. All the way home, that book held the same urgent appeal to me as a lifeboat has to a person on a sinking ship. I couldn't wait to get into it. I still felt that my intelligence had been insulted by the title, but something deeper inside me was excited, and I wasn't sure why.

Once inside my door, I immediately kicked off my shoes, sat down at my kitchen table, opened that book and began to read. I soon found that the book had been written for people who live with alcoholics, to teach them how to try to cope in the midst of the insanity, and to show them the reasons they'd been drawn to alcoholics in the FIRST place. Oh, my gosh, I thought, this book really IS for me! My resentment subsiding, I continued to read. I was just in the first chapter when I read something so enlightening that I began to laugh with unexpected joy. I now felt like a little kid who has just opened the most surprisingly wonderful gift from a loving parent. All I said at that point was "Lord, You GAVE me this book, didn't you!" I was thrilled because now I knew that the drawing to this book had been in answer to my prayer for understanding.

He corrected me with His answer to my exclamation. "No, Vicki," He responded, "I didn't give you this book. You bought it yourself. All I did was lead you to it." He's SUCH a stickler for details! By the time I had finished this little book, I completely understood why I had always been drawn to alcoholics. I had developed a mental pattern that enabled me to survive while growing up with my father. The book had gone into magnificent detail about what happens when you've grown up with an alcoholic at home, the mental patterns that you form as a result, and how those patterns control your life. The right knowledge really DOES empower. The power that it held was the power to change ME, and the way I understood life. I live in an area where alcoholism is a predominant problem, so I've lived around many women who have to deal with this problem all the time. Men are not exempt from this problem, either.

We don't consciously choose to live in ridiculous circumstances, but we WILL be drawn to the very things we need to overcome. There were Christians who would ask me why I stayed in a marriage that was so difficult, but any time I wanted to leave, the Lord would say to me "Stay where you are". I didn't want to stay, but in spite of the fact that I wanted to leave, I had a stronger conviction, and that was to obey God's instruction.

To add to the dilemma, each time I wanted to leave I'd receive a call or a card from a Christian acquaintance, telling me that they'd been awakened in the night to pray for me, or that they had been led to pray for me on their way to work, etc., and that God's message to me was that I was safe in His care, and that I was right where He wanted me to be. The amazing thing about that, was that the people who would call didn't know me all that well, and had no idea what my situation WAS. What I didn't understand yet was that God had a greater plan for me than I could have imagined. He told me once, that by the time we got through this, I'd never be drawn to an alcoholic again. Of course, my thought on that was that I'd probably be dead from this experience, and I wouldn't have to worry about being drawn to ANYONE!

Joyce and I prayed often during our daily prayer time concerning my circumstances, especially during a very dark three-year period, but each time the same answer came, "Stay where you are". As time went on, although the circumstances became seemingly unbearable, I had finally quit asking the Lord's permission to leave, and surrendered to my fate. My final surrender came the day I decided that if I actually got killed in this situation, and someone would somehow benefit from my death, then it was okay with me. As it turned out, that's exactly what happened, but in a way I'd never thought of. The seriousness of my situation kept driving me to God in prayer, simply for survival. What I didn't realize was happening, was that each time I went to Him, and He would replace my thoughts with His thoughts, and my attitudes with His, my old self really was dying, and God's truth was becoming stronger and stronger in me. Then one evening, the strength of God rose up from deep within me, and I said "Enough! I don't have to live like this any more, and I won't!" That night I left there, and stayed with my daughter for a few days. It was so peaceful there that I knew I'd never go back to that nonsense again that I had just left. After all that time, I finally knew I was worth more than this, and it was the greatest feeling on earth. A power from deep within me had risen to the occasion, and thrown off all of the intimidation I had previously been under. It was finally gone. The old thought pattern had finally been broken in the deepest part of me in this area, and I had actually felt the change, deep down inside, in the split second that it had taken place. The end result? My husband quit drinking, and I went home...for a while.

My husband kept trying to tell me that he would never drink again, but I'd heard this all before, and I wasn't going to trust this statement one more time. I'd believed it so many times before, only to finally let my guard down, and end up in another shock wave when the alcoholic insanity would strike again. I was no longer able to believe in anyone's good intentions. But he didn't drink, and weeks were going by, and although he was quite proud of his accomplishment, I was becoming more and more stressed. No one could tell me that this wasn't just another trick, because that's exactly what I believed it was. I ended up walking out of there again for a short period of time, and this time EVERYONE was upset with me, because they couldn't understand why I'd wanted him to quit drinking for so long, then, when he DID, I left! I didn't really understand it myself, until I questioned the Lord about it later.

He informed me that I was suffering from a type of " culture shock". As much as I had wanted the insanity out of our lives, alcoholism was what I had lived with, from the time I was a child. The lack of it, although highly desired, was unfamiliar to me, and I wasn't sure how to cope. Also, I really didn't believe the change was permanent. I had spent too many times believing that the nightmare was over, only to have my hopes crushed again by another drunken attack. When the drinking really DID stop, I had kept my guard up, believing that if I let it down again, I'd be hit with yet another wave, and I knew I'd never survive one more time of this kind of shock. Since I couldn't believe that sobriety would last, each day that went by only caused me to believe that we were one day closer to the crash again, and the stress of waiting for another failure became too much for me to live with. I left again, totally convinced that the recurring nightmare was surely just around the corner.

When I took flight this time, it was to save what little sanity I thought I had left, believing that as soon as I was out the door, he'd be right back to the bars again. Much to my surprise, he wasn't. The day came when he and I had a conversation, in which he stated "You're not going to MAKE me drink again, no matter WHAT you do." It was at that moment that I knew inside that he was really done with that saturated lifestyle. I was finally able to let my guard down without fear of another crash.

Earlier I compared a life under the influence of alcohol to a roller coaster ride, and I still understand it that way. It doesn't matter if it's you under the influence, or someone else who's taken the ride and dragged you along with them. The fact is, the ups and downs of the ride itself throws you so completely off balance that when the ride really stops for good, and you're finally able to get off, it's still going to take a while for you to get your balance. So if any of you have prayed for this ride to stop, be very kind to yourself when it does. Take it easy for a while. The shock of an abrupt ending can send you into another kind of spinning that can cause you to take a serious fall. But even if you do fall in the dizziness of the aftermath, don't be hard on yourself. You'll regain your balance soon enough, and be able to move forward in your life.

A whole new set of problems came to the forefront now. I had learned to use being a victim of alcoholism as an excuse for my own shortcomings. Now that the drinking had stopped, and I no longer had to live under that type of stress, I'd have to own up to the fact that my shortcomings were because of ME! It was time now to deal with the things in ME that were still causing me problems. I had thought that when I no longer had to deal with alcoholism in my home, that my life would take off like a rocket. However, I was still stalling out, so I began an even deeper search with God to discover whatever misconceptions I still had imbedded in me that were still holding me back from enjoying the life that God promises to all of His children. I had grown up on a roller coaster ride that had caused me to view life at such an emotionally jolting pace, that the mental pictures that I had taken along the way, of myself and life in general, were pretty blurred. Now I was ready to begin a fascinating part of this journey that would allow God to go after those distorted images that I carried in my mental photo album, and let Him replace those blurred images with clear shots of who I really was, from His point of view.

chapter 17
EYES FOR THE JOURNEY

I'm sure you've heard the phrase "A picture is worth a thousand words." A picture is an invaluable tool for accuracy. Have you ever had someone describe something to you, then you've actually seen that "something" later, only to exclaim "Wow! I never would have pictured this! I pictured it so differently!"? Another way to show the value of a picture is to have a half-dozen people sit around a table while you describe something for them to draw. Will any of their pictures be the same? Not likely! The reason they'd be so varied, is because while we are hearing the description, our imaginations kick in, and form their OWN version of what's described.

For instance, the color blue is mentioned, and each person's imagination takes hold of a different shade of blue, according to individual preference, or experience. BUT, what if you held up the picture of what you're describing, while you talk about it. Now when the color blue is mentioned, everyone sees the same color blue as the one who made the picture. I've always found it helpful to see a picture of something, THEN read how the author describes how he wants you to see it. When I see the picture first, I get a more accurate account of what the author is talking about. I'm now able to see through the author's eyes, without the aid of my sometimes inaccurate imagination. One evening, while we still had the alcohol problem at home, I was introduced to a NEW form of pictures, one that would allow me to see more accurately what God, the Author, wanted me to see. This is just one example of many, to show how God used a difficult situation to force me to grow.

My husband's drinking had escalated again, and when it did, he would no longer be in charge of himself, but the rage that was in him would take over, which would generally lead to violence. By this particular evening, the mood in my home had become treacherous. This latest "spree "was lasting for days. While I nervously waited to see what he'd be like when he got home, I received a phone call from one of my step-daughters. She had recently moved back to town. She and I had formed a very close bond since she had given her life to God, and she wanted me to come and visit. She'd already heard how heavily her dad had been drinking, and she finally confessed to me that she really wanted me to come and spend the night, just to ease her mind. That idea became quite appealing as we talked, since we always had so much to share about the Lord. I accepted her invitation, relieved to not have to witness a black mood again tonight. I called Joyce to let her know where I'd be in case she tried to call, and drove to the other end of town.

I hadn't been at my step-daughter's apartment long, when Joyce showed up, too. She said she'd come to take me out somewhere for dessert and coffee, or even just for a drive together, just to take my mind off the tension that had been going on at home. We considered that , but while the three of us talked, we came up with a far more intriguing idea. Why not have an all night prayer meeting? Hmmmm...dessert and coffee, or an evening with God in prayer? We declared "No Contest!", and opted for the prayer. This would be like a Christian pajama party, we mused, only without the pajamas. Just the thought of a meeting like that, without restrictions on our time, brought an attitude of relaxed adventure to all of us. A couple of Christian neighbors that we had spent time with in a Bible study, dropped by, and they thought it was a wonderful idea and wanted to join us, although, they said, they wouldn't be able to stay all night. No problem.

The Bible says that the Lord is a rewarder of those who diligently seek Him, and I was about to find that out. About an hour into the prayer time, during a quiet moment, one of the ladies mentioned something that she was having a problem with, and needed to pray about. To this day, I couldn't tell you what it was that was bothering her. Before she had even brought this up, the most interesting thing was already happening with me.

While my eyes were closed, I could see a small group of little girls holding hands, and dancing around in a circle, at the foot of what appeared to be a throne. As the lady at the table began to pray, I saw one little girl in the circle, let go of the other girls' hands, walk to the foot of the throne, and kneel there. She bowed her head. As the lady stopped praying, I watched that same little girl stand up, turn around, and walk back to the circle and join in again. I said nothing, but sat there with my eyes closed, watching those little girls, still dancing around in their circle.

Then I heard someone else begin to pray. As she began, I watched another little girl leave the circle, and walk to the foot of the throne, and kneel. She bowed her head, just like the other girl had done. I watched this scene three times, as three different ladies prayed. Then I counted. There were five little girls dancing in that circle, while the same number of ladies prayed at the table. I was so caught up in what I was seeing, that I hadn't realized how quiet I'd become while everyone else prayed. My silence had been noticed by the others, however, and they asked now WHY I'd been so quiet. Without opening my eyes, I answered by asking them to please continue, because there was something really neat going on from where I sat. I told them that it was as though I was watching a movie with my eyes closed. It seemed as though I was watching them pray, with a whole new way of seeing it. They continued to pray, and I continued to watch. When the prayer was finished, the vision went away. When it was gone, I opened my eyes and began to describe to the others every detail of what I had just watched, right down to the ruffles on the dresses that the little girls were wearing.

None of us had any idea what had just taken place, because none of us had ever experienced anything like this before. The neighbors had already left when we decided to go back to God about this strange experience. We asked what this was that had happened, and the Lord answered by saying to me, "You have no idea the power source that you have just tapped into". Wanting to know if this was good or bad, since it was still a mystery, we continued in prayer, asking why it had happened. He answered by adding, "Because of your faithfulness in prayer". And that was all He had to say that night about it, and the rest of the time that we were able to stay up that night, we spent in prayers of gratitude for who He is, for all His love, and now for this new power source that He said we had tapped into.

We could have done so many things with our time that night, but we had chosen to spend the time seeking God. We hadn't gone into the prayer expecting anything other than the chance to talk with Him, but He rewarded us with something amazing, something we didn't know existed for us. He always gives us so much more than we expect. He honored our choice, and rewarded us all, by beginning a whole new chapter for us. You see, even though I was the one who had "watched the movie", it didn't take long for the others who desired to see as the Holy Spirit sees, to ask God to open up their spiritual eyes, too.

We can't ask for things that we don't even know exist. Once I'd read a book about a man who could see things in the spirit, but I had just thought he was "special". What I hadn't realized back then is that we're ALL special, the power and gifts of the Holy Spirit are available to ALL of God's kids. Once we understand this, we can ask for the gifts of the Spirit to be made available to us, and as we ask, and blocks are removed, we receive. That night in prayer was just the beginning of finding out about resources we had at hand, as a prayer group, through the power of the Holy Spirit.

The times of "seeing" became more frequent as time went on, until we learned to expect to see what was needed to be seen. It was a classic example of God re-conditioning us. We no longer had to rely on our limited understanding to show us what we needed to know. We could now tap into the realm of the spirit, where all things are seen more clearly, from God's point of view. We have a supernatural Father who desires His children to live according to His power, not man's. He has supernatural power to reveal and to heal, and He wants to share that power with His kids. He will share it, once we know it's there, that is, and when we learn to ask. Or, as in our case, just because we chose time with Him over any other activity.

Well, this had certainly been an interesting evening, to say the least, and I discovered when all was said and done, that I wasn't even upset about my husband any more. I actually entertained the thought of thanking him that things had gotten bad enough to make me leave for the evening. Good grief, look what had happened out of it! If the situation hadn't gotten that bad, I would have spent a peaceful evening at home, but I was so thrilled about the outcome of the evening, how could I possibly be upset with the one who had helped me get there? I did end up sleeping at my stepdaughter's apartment that night, but when I went home the next morning all was peaceful again, and remained that way for quite some time. I may have, out of apprehension, been driven elsewhere for the night, but who cared? I'd brought a fantastic new gift back home with me when I returned.

chapter 18
INCOMING!

I began to feel a deep, quiet nagging about starting a Bible study in my home. I didn't exactly HEAR from God about it, as much as I knew deep down inside that it was time. Joyce and I went to God about this, and the peace came only when we inquired about Thursdays. So Thursdays it would be. We didn't have peace with the following Thursday, though, so we left it with God as to which Thursday would be the first. It was a month later when the meetings actually got started. Others had been notified as to when the meetings would begin, and they were coming, so I was getting excited about everyone getting together.

Finally the day arrived when we would have our first meeting in the house. I spent the day thanking God for this opportunity, while I busied myself putting the house in order for company in the evening. We had a seven-o'clock meeting planned, and there was much to do. I had everything ready and the coffee was on by six-thirty, which gave me time to sit down with my Bible and read a while before anyone else arrived. Seven o'clock came and went, and no one was there yet, but people are late for a lot of things, so I didn't worry about it. I just continued to read by myself while I waited. By 7:30, I was becoming a little puzzled as to why no one was there yet, but what I was reading was keeping me happy, so I remained at the table, and continued on.

Eight o'clock came, and by now I was thinking that it was strange that even Joyce wasn't there yet, so I thought I'd better call and see if everything was okay with her. No answer. She must be on her way finally, but I wondered what was keeping the others. By eight-thirty I was pretty sure that Joyce wasn't coming, since I'd called a half-hour ago, and she only lived about three minutes from my house. Wasn't this strange? And where was everyone else? Oh well, I would finish reading this chapter, I decided, and I could worry about it later.

By nine o'clock I began questioning what had happened here tonight, "Where is everyone, Lord? I know tonight's the night we're to begin this study, so what's going on?"

"They're not coming," He said quietly, then added "so what are you going to do?"

I began thinking that there wasn't much use in having a Bible study here, if no one was going to come. What a disappointment this was! I couldn't imagine why I had felt so strongly about this, and I even knew the day it was to begin. Everyone else had been excited about it too, and then no one showed up. Not even Joyce, and she had helped PLAN it! Had I completely missed God on this one?

"Well, Lord," I began again "this was definitely a disaster."

"What disaster took place?" He inquired, causing me to re-think my phrase.

"Well, there wasn't any HARM done, actually," I had to admit.

"What did you expect to have happen here tonight?", He went on.

"Lord, You know I was expecting to have a Bible study." Why, I wondered, was He asking these silly questions, when He already KNEW what I was expecting.

"And did you have one?" He asked.

"What do you mean, did I have one? You KNOW nobody…" I stopped abruptly, and smiled, finally beginning to get His point.

"Yes, Lord, as a matter of fact, I did." It was all becoming kind of humorous now, and I couldn't help but chuckle.

"And did you enjoy it?" He prodded me on to even more awareness.

"Yes, Lord, I did!" I was laughing out loud now at the way the evening had turned out, and by the way the Lord was leading this conversation.

"Then what will you do?" He asked again, and I realized that we had just gone full circle, back to His original question.

As I sat there thinking about the evening, and all that I had EXPECTED to happen, and what had actually happened instead, I had to admit that I had completely enjoyed the time that I had spent, and so what, if no one else had come. I had had a great time. It was at this time that I understood what He was asking, and it was at this time also, that I knew what my answer would be.

"Lord," I began again, "You let me know that it was time to start a Bible study here, and so it's been started. I will continue this study, even if it is by myself, for as long as You want it. Every Thursday evening is set aside for this study, and don't worry, Lord, if no one else ever comes to join me, it doesn't matter. I'll be here."

And that's the way the meetings began that night, with me making a decision to do what I was led to do, no matter what. Joyce called later that night to tell me that she couldn't believe it, but it's as if the whole evening plan had been erased from her mind, and she and her husband had gone elsewhere for the evening. She never remembered at all that we were having the meeting tonight, until right now. She was so apologetic and so disappointed to have missed it, but I assured her it had been a wonderful evening, and added that I was sorry she couldn't make it. She was shocked when she asked who all had been there, and I answered "no one, just me."

The following Thursday evening I was sitting at my table with my Bible again. Approximately ten minutes before seven, Joyce arrived. At seven, she and I opened the meeting with prayer, and the two of us had a marvelous Bible study, followed by more prayer. The Thursday after that, she and I were joined by someone else, so then there were three. Each week another would be added, until we had to move more chairs into the kitchen, because the eight, then ten, then twelve, that were already set up there were not enough.

The group that met together in my home continued to steadily increase, until the time came when it was not unusual to find three rooms fully occupied every Thursday evening. Everyone was welcome, and everyone was important. We had such a variety of people, from business owners, to construction workers who were in town only for a short time, to people who were so wounded that they couldn't even THINK of getting their lives together yet. People came from different churches, just to check us out, for meetings like this in our area were something new.

When something is new, the fearful will criticize. When you're doing something right, the enemy attacks. When rumors fly, the bravest will come to see what all the fuss is about. What they found there was a common thread that connected us all, and that was our love for God and for one another, which included them.

What we were experiencing there was full-body ministry, where everyone gave and everyone received, according to whatever they had, or needed. Lives change, however, and people eventually move on, but the kinship that took place between us all back then has always remained a wonderfully warm memory. We always look back with gratitude to God for the love that was there, and the power of the Holy Spirit that forged it.

There was a freedom in those meetings for everyone to move as they were led by the Holy Spirit, who was in charge. There was an order and a comfortableness about the meetings. We were a combination of church, school, and spiritual hospital.

I shudder to think what I would have missed if the Lord hadn't talked me through the first night. I wouldn't have been punished in any way if I had stopped the meetings because nobody came, but oh, the blessings and the friendships that would have been missed. At one time, we came to jokingly call ourselves a "M.A.S.H. Unit" because of the amount of spiritually wounded coming in. We ourselves had been so wounded, and God had allowed us to open up a place where He could be Teacher, Counselor, and Physician.

There were no time limits there. The meetings began around seven. They lasted until whatever needed to be done, was done. If the meeting ended by eleven, we came to consider it an early night. Many times one or two in the morning would find us finally saying goodnight. If you couldn't get there until nine, that was fine. If you worked until eleven, you could join us after that. Each person left when they felt the unction to go, but no one ever left there without receiving individual prayer. It was an open house, with God in charge.

There were many times that we would be so caught up in studying together, counseling together, and praying together, that when someone would happen to look at the clock, and announce that it was after midnight already, we'd be shocked. We'd all agree that it seemed like we'd just gotten started. Everyone who came received individual attention. The wounded need a place to be where they can receive the unconditional love they need, in order to gather the strength they need to try again.

Life is about change, and we all move on eventually. Our group was no exception to this rule. People came, stayed as long as they needed to be with us, and then they'd move on, according to wherever God led them. We had no ownership problems with anyone, and thank God, they had no ownership issues with us. We had one authority figure that we wanted to please, and that was Jesus Christ. When people came, we loved them. When they moved on, we wished them well. That's the way it should be, freedom for each child of God to move ahead on their path as they are led by the Spirit of God.

chapter 19
A MIRACLE IN FEATHERS

I mentioned earlier that my second husband and I had moved into the "homestead". This was the old house that he and his siblings had lived in for most of their growing-up years. My husband had bought it from his father shortly before we married. That house had weathered many a storm over the years, inside and out, until it gave the appearance of an old weather-worn farmhouse, rather than a typical house sitting among others on a residential tree-lined street.

I always wondered if the appearance of the house was what prompted one of my step-daughters to bring an occasional barn-yard "surprise" for her dad. She and her family lived on a farm outside a neighboring town, and every now and then she would show up with one of these surprises. Once, she brought a large white goose that lived with us for months. Another time, she showed up with a goat, the size of a large dog. It always took me a while to get used to these farm animals, but once I'd get over the shock, I'd be okay. The goose hadn't really made much of an impression on me, so I'd had no problem with it being eventually given to someone who lived more in a country setting. It would be happier with other geese, anyway....right? The goat was a different story entirely.

I wasn't at all interested, at first, in having a GOAT on the property, but I couldn't help getting attached to it. He WAS more like a big dog, and just as friendly. He quickly became a comical addition to the family. A goat really wasn't appropriate for where we lived, however, and after having him with us for months, he was transferred to a farm where he could live with other goats.

A MIRACLE IN FEATHERS

As much as I really didn't want to be running a farm myself, I cried all night the night he left. He had become my pet.

The most memorable of all the "surprises" arrived on a beautiful summer afternoon while I was on the other end of town, grocery shopping. I arrived home to find my step-daughter's car in the driveway, and I smiled. She's one of the sweetest people I've ever met, and it was nice to see that she and her family had come to visit. They were all in the back yard when I got home, and they hadn't noticed my arrival yet. This was perfect, I thought, because I could get the groceries put away, and put on a pot of coffee before they'd even know I was here. These visits always ended the same way, with everyone sitting around the kitchen table for coffee and more conversation.

I had the situation well under control...or so I thought. I had put about three cans in a cupboard when my eight-year old step-grandson came bursting through the door, his face flushed and his eyes gleaming.

"Vicki!" he was gasping for air from running the length of the yard "everybody's outside! Are you coming out?" The twinkle in his eyes seemed to increase as he continued "We brought you and Grampa a surprise!"

"Uh, oh!" I immediately went into "RED-ALERT", but just as quickly, I composed myself outwardly, in order not to alarm this excited little boy. After all, the fact that they had brought me and Grampa something didn't necessarily mean it would be something I'd have to feed and be responsible for, did it?

"And what would that surprise be?" I inquired casually, all the while aware of a distinctly uneasy feeling, much like dread, forming deep down inside me. I continued to put the groceries away while we talked.

"I can't tell you! It's a SURPRISE! You gotta come out! Are you coming out now?" He was jumping up and down in his excitement, and I could see that he was having a really hard time containing the news.

Now, I believe that a person should always be honest with children, but there are times when a situation will arise that warrants other tactics. I could see that this was going to be one of those times, so I did the only thing that any red-blooded, panic-influenced person would do. I conned the truth out of him.

I bent down closer to him and forced a twinkle in my eyes that would almost match the twinkle in his. " Can't you just give me a hint?"

"I CAN'T!" His eyes were widening under the pressure. It seemed as though he were going to burst! "It's a SURPRISE!"

"I'll tell you what," I said, "I have to finish putting these few things away first before I can come out." The look on his face as he shot a look at the bags gave a silent message that he'd NEVER be able to wait that long, so I continued softly, "But if you tell me what the surprise is, I promise I won't tell anyone that you told me, and I promise I'll act so surprised when they tell me what it is, that no one would ever guess. It will just be our little secret, okay? How would THAT be?"

This was something he considered for approximately four seconds before he decided that this would work. "Okay." he said with a solemn, decision-making nod of his head. We had hit upon a solution to his dilemma. I could finish putting these things away, and he wouldn't have to burst in the waiting. Gosh, I had already made him wait nearly a minute, and it had been agonizing for him. A secret is much too heavy a burden for an eight year old to bear for any length of time, after all, and they are so relieved to rid themselves of that burden.

"Well?" I prodded him one last time.

He broke into the biggest smile that a little boy's face can produce, while he triumphantly announced "It's a TURKEY!"

I FROZE! I mustered up enough courage to ask one question that could turn this situation from horror to happiness. "Is it in the freezer?"

"Nope!" He finalized the blow. " It's walking around in the back yard, and it's a BIG one!" he beamed. With that said, he turned to bolt back out the kitchen door, stopped, turned, and momentarily reassured himself with, "You PROMISE not to tell them I told you?"

"I promise." My answer was firm.

I heard him yelling all the way to the back of the yard, "She'll be out in a minute!" He had bolted back to the yard as quickly as he had bolted in, and no sooner had the screen door slammed behind him, than I had collapsed onto one of the kitchen chairs in what could only be called a full-blown panic attack. "Oh, God," I gasped, "this can NOT be happening again!" I had been a little apprehensive before, with the other animals, but this time it was different. THIS time, I felt an actual RAGE bubble up inside me, as though a dam had broken and I was about to drown from within. I don't remember ever being that overwhelmed before. I was so overwhelmed, that I couldn't say anything more than "GOD... What will I DO? GOD, WHAT WILL I DO?"

For lack of knowing what else to do, I hurled myself into my prayer language. I was in one awful inner battle right then, with no way out that I could see. To my amazement, within about ten seconds of the prayer, that fury that had completely enveloped me, disappeared, just as instantly as it had come. What had just happened here? I wasn't sure, but I was certainly relieved. I was back to normal, and I knew that the Spirit of God within me had just waged war with SOMETHING, and WON!

Being suddenly calm, I still wasn't happy about having a live turkey in the yard, so I said "Lord, why a TURKEY? I don't live on a farm, and I don't WANT to own a turkey!"

The Lord soothed me right then with a very gentle statement concerning the situation. "Don't be upset. I have a plan for this turkey."

Well, this statement set my mind to racing. After all, hadn't we had other animals brought here before? And hadn't they ended up going to farms? Immediately I imagined the plan. We would keep the turkey for a little while, then it would be time to take it to a farm, and the farmer probably didn't even KNOW the Lord yet, so I'd be able to talk to him and share the love of Jesus with him, and his life would be changed forever, and all was suddenly RIGHT with my world. I calmly got up from the table, put the rest of the groceries away, and went outside with a very warm smile. I was looking forward now to meeting this new instrument of God. This time, I was the one with the secret.

We had that turkey for at least a year, and although Tony was the one who tended to him, any time I was around him, I looked at him with excitement, knowing that God had a plan for him.

Our Bible study meetings were still going strong, and during this time we had moved the meetings to Joyce's. She and her husband owned a local bar/restaurant, and had become swamped at lunch time every day, so I had gone to work for them for a couple of hours each weekday, to help handle the overload. We had a great time working together, because we were constantly talking about the things the Lord was doing in our lives.

On one particular meeting night, as we began to pray, the Lord said he was giving each one a gift As we waited, he spoke to each one concerning what they were to expect. When they prayed for me, I heard one word....Miracles. Oh, no! I associated miracles with those people who are on a stage praying for people and they're miraculously healed, and everyone is watching every move they make. To say the LEAST, they're the center of attention.

"I don't WANT to do miracles, Lord. I don't WANT to be the center of attention." I was really getting nervous about this. "Couldn't I just have something the whole world wouldn't know about?"

"Trust me", was all he had to say.

A few days later I was washing the dinner dishes, when my husband came rushing through the kitchen mumbling something about the turkey. He and his brother had been out in the back yard that evening talking with some friends who had stopped by the house after dinner. I hadn't heard what he'd said other than "turkey", so I asked him to repeat it. He told me that the turkey must have gotten a cut on his leg, or maybe he'd been bitten by something, they weren't sure, but by the time the injury had become noticeable, gangrene had already set in. He said his brother had checked it, and confirmed that's what it was. Tony was upset, but I was even more upset by this news. The turkey wasn't exactly my pet, but I had known God had a plan for it for so long, that I had developed a type of protective attitude toward it.

"Vick, we can't keep him with his leg like that. He would suffer. My brother will come and get him tomorrow and take care of everything.. You won't even be here when he comes. You'll be at work by then, so you won't have to worry about it." With that, he went back out to join the others.

I was so stunned by what I had just heard, I went straight to the living room and fell into the nearest chair. "Lord!" I said, "Did you hear what he SAID? They're going to kill the turkey! This can't be HAPPENING! We haven't even MET the farmer yet!" My mind had immediately gone back to the day the Lord had said to me "I have a plan for the turkey". Then I calmed inside and went on "Lord, that's what THEY'VE said. What do YOU have to say?"

His answer was calm and quiet. "You lay hands on the turkey," He said, "and I will heal him."

"What?" I thought I hadn't heard right.

"You lay hands on the turkey," He repeated, "and I will heal him". Oh, My Gosh! THANK YOU, Lord. I was so relieved to hear this, I jumped right up out of that chair, happy again.

All of a sudden a new problem came to mind. The fact was that I didn't have the nerve to go out there in front of people and pray for a turkey. My heart sank, knowing that I didn't have the courage to do this in front of anyone, and feeling like my self-consciousness would surely be pronouncing a death sentence on a harmless creature. "Those guys are all out there. Do I have to do this NOW?"

He very gently responded with, "I didn't say when. I said if you lay hands on the turkey, I will heal him." I was so grateful to hear this. I knew I needed privacy to pray for the turkey. Besides, in the morning my husband would leave for work, then I'd have time to get ready for work myself, then I could go pray for the turkey before my sister-in-law came to pick me up for work. This would work. There'd be no one around, and I'd have the privacy I needed.

In the morning, everything went like clockwork. I still had about twenty minutes before my sister-in-law came to pick me up, and I was ready to go. I had straightened the house, and had my reading time and I'd left ample time to pray for the turkey. That was my plan. That was all fine and dandy until I got to the shed. I opened the door, stepped inside, and then it hit me. Lay HANDS on the turkey. "Oh, Lord, I hadn't realized what you were asking me to do! I'm going to have to actually TOUCH this turkey?" I guess, when He had said 'lay hands on the turkey', I had interpreted that as go and PRAY for him. Uh, oh,! I had a problem now for SURE. I couldn't bear the thought of touching this bird. Other pets you can pet and hold and snuggle, usually. I had called the turkey a pet, but he wasn't ever my idea of something I wanted to pet, or even get that CLOSE to, for that matter. I considered turkeys to be really strange looking creatures, and although I'd gotten used to him, and cared about him, touching him was something I could never bring myself to do. I had always been content to enjoy him from afar. Now, SUDDENLY, I'm faced with a problem. God had specifically said "Lay hands on the turkey", and now I couldn't imagine how I was going to TOUCH this bird while I prayed for it. Oh, man, this just wasn't going to be as easy as I had thought.

I must have been a riotous sight in God's eyes that morning while I wrestled with the situation. I'd take a deep breath, step close to the turkey, try to touch it, it would move, and I'd run right out of the shed. Then I'd have to calm down, go back into that shed, and try again. I ended up doing this about four times, when I looked up the street and saw my sister-in-law coming across the bridge. "OH, NO!" I screamed inside, "I'm out of time! I have to do this now, or the turkey's going to be killed! God, HELP me!" I looked over my shoulder and sure enough, Joyce was pulling into the driveway.

With all the courage I could muster with one last deep breath, I stepped into the shed one more time, stood behind the turkey, and with one hand positioned in the air on either side of him, I squeezed my eyes shut as I forced my hands to make contact with those feathers. I no sooner made contact, than he gobbled, and the hair on the back of my neck stood straight up as a repulsed chill went right through me. My hands recoiled faster than they had ever moved before, and I flew out of the shed and shut the door behind me. I couldn't do any more, and I knew it. I was so repulsed by the experience of touching that turkey, that I gave up. I threw my hands up in the air. "THERE! I DID IT! I TOUCHED him!" I exclaimed, exasperated. "I'm sorry, Lord, I just can't DO this!"

I was crumbling now inside, feeling that I had just disappointed God, and the turkey, but I had also become all-too-aware of my own limitations. As I walked across the yard, defeated, to go to Joyce's car, I heard again, "You lay hands on the turkey, and I'll heal him." Startled, I brightened. "Lord," I said, "You didn't TELL me to pray for the turkey. You just said 'lay hands on him' , and I DID. I touched him with BOTH HANDS! I DID my part. Now the rest is up to YOU."

Joyce roared with laughter as we drove to work and I told her what had happened, but she said the same thing I had said. "The rest is up to God."

We had a really busy time at work that day, and when the lunch rush was over I busied myself with clearing off tables , washing glasses, and generally putting things back in order. I was behind the bar washing glasses when I heard a familiar voice talking above the clatter. I had been so busy with the tables that I hadn't seen my brother-in law come in, the same brother-in-law who was to take the turkey that morning. He was talking quite animatedly to two men, one on either side of him. I began to catch bits and pieces of his conversation while I continued to wash the glasses.

"I'm TELLING you, that turkey had gangrene in it's leg. We were over there last night, and I saw it myself. I know for a FACT that's what it had. But, when I went there this morning... I'm TELLING you, that turkey had gangrene in its leg last night, and today there's nothing wrong with it. I've never seen anything like it!"

I stopped washing glasses and walked quietly back to the kitchen, stunned again. Joyce was cleaning up her end of the lunchtime mess, and the look of awe on my face told her something had happened. I told her what our brother-in-law had been telling those men out at the bar, and we both took a moment to be in awe.

I didn't have to check on the turkey when I got home that day. I knew he was fine now. I didn't need to see his leg. I already knew from my brother-in-law's conversation that God had done exactly what he'd said He would do. I never felt the need to say anything to anyone, other than my husband, and our prayer group, about what had happened. This was like a sacred event, between me and my Father. I never needed to check on what He'd done, for I'd already heard what He had done.. I didn't need to "see for myself", for someone else had seen. I didn't get over the awe of that for a long, long time. As a matter of fact, just writing about it now brings the same awesome reverence for a God who would do something like that.

Oh, by the way, I never did meet the farmer I always thought I'd meet because of the turkey, but when I questioned the Lord about that once, He said "I never said anything about a farmer. That was what you assumed would happen. I told you I would use the turkey. I also told you that I would give you miracles, and you were afraid of that. I used the turkey to show you what a miracle consists of. You brought the problem to me. I told you what I wanted you to do, then I told you what I would do. I told you if you would lay hands on the turkey, I would heal him. It was an agreement between us. You did what I asked, and I did what I promised. It's really that simple, but this is what what men call "miracles".

chapter 20
THE ANONYMOUS CARD

A wounded self-image creates self-consciousness.
Self-conscious people are forever trying to hide from the limelight,
because they don't want others to see the hideous flaws that they,
themselves, believe they have. I had a BIG problem with self-consciousness before I was healed. I HATED having to be the center
of attention for any reason. It was because of this self-consciousness, that I had to depend on God for anything I was asked to
do in the monthly Full-Gospel meetings I attended. One morning,
before one of those meetings was to begin, I was asked to take
charge of the prayer before the offering was taken. I panicked, of
course, thinking that I didn't want to get up in front of others and
lead ANYTHING. It was bad enough, I thought, that I had to sit
at a head table, in front of everyone else, with the other board
members, because I was the treasurer.

In my panic, I went straight to the Lord with my fear, told Him
I was stepping aside and asked the Holy Spirit, who I knew resided
in me, to lead the discussion and prayer, instead of me. This gave
me the confidence to step up to the front of the room when
it was time for me to take over. I was familiar with scriptures
everyone used concerning tithing and giving, but I was uneasy
about those scriptures this morning, and didn't want to use them.
I just kept feeling that there must be more to giving than just
focusing on money.

What the Holy Spirit brought out that morning was as enlightening to me at that time, as it may have been to others in the
room. He ended up pointing out that when God says give, He's
NOT just talking about money. He's talking about giving of yourself in any situation, such as giving a smile or an encouraging word

when it's needed, or giving your time to help someone. What we focused on that morning, was that when you give ANYTHING, give with a joyful heart, because when you do, you are then able to receive, pressed down, shaken together, and running over. Give whatever God shows you is needed, for you don't know when you're going to be in adverse circumstances yourself, and have need of someone giving to you.

It was shortly after that, that I was walking home from working with my sister-in-law, serving lunches over the noon hour again. I was halfway home when I saw a brief vision of my own hands putting a ten-dollar bill inside a "Thinking-of-You" card. That vision was impressed on me twice while I was walking home. The strange part of the vision was that I knew who the card was to be sent to, and I knew that it was to be sent anonymously, and there was a scripture reference that was to be written on the inside of it, referring to the fact that God supplies all of our need. Although I knew who was to receive the card, and I knew who these people were to see them, I didn't PERSONALLY know them, or anything about their circumstances.

I had some cards at home, so that wouldn't be a problem. I didn't know where these people lived, but the phone book provided that information. I used my Bible Concordance to locate the scripture reference, and wrote the reference inside the card I had found. When the card and envelope were ready, I took my wallet out of my purse to get the money that was to be inserted. When I opened my wallet, I found a ten-dollar bill and a five-dollar bill inside. That was it. Nothing more. I suddenly realized that this was all the money that I would have until the next payday, and I immediately saw a sorry situation here. If I put the ten-dollar bill in the card, that would leave me with a scrawny, little five dollars left to my name. I actually said at that moment "Wow, Lord, I'm a little short on cash here. Would it be alright if I just put the five in?"

The vision flashed again, and again I saw the ten-dollar bill go inside the card. Okay, ten dollars it would be. I slipped the money inside the card, sealed it, and started walking back toward town. I had time to get to the post office and back before it was time to begin making dinner. No one besides myself and God ever knew that ever happened. I didn't dare tell anyone else, for to me anonymous meant that it was a secret between me and God. I was inwardly thrilled, because I knew that I had just been permitted to be a part of building someone's faith, and that always brings about a deep, deep joy.

Over a year later, Tony and I were going through a very interesting financial situation. My husband, being a roofer, only worked when the weather was good. He had been laid off for the winter again, and something had gone wrong with his unemployment checks that we had to depend on through the winter months. We found out later that someone had made a mistake in paperwork, and his checks had been sent to a wrong address. We didn't find out what had happened though, until about six weeks later, when they were recovered. During that six-week period, there was no income for our household. I wasn't working with my sister-in-law any longer, because the lunch-time rush had subsided. My husband had gone looking for any type of temporary work in the meantime, but nothing seemed to be available.

Joyce and I had enrolled in a home-study course from a Bible College just prior to this, and we were totally absorbed in learning even more about the power of the Holy Spirit, so I really had no time or energy to devote to worrying, while this was happening. I was so caught up in what I was learning, that I gave little-to-no thought to the financial crisis that was forming, while I remained focused on God.

We had used up everything in the house as far as food was concerned, and there certainly wasn't any money for ANYTHING else by now. The household bills sat unpaid, and there was no way to put gas in the truck any more. We had become, for the most part, penniless. If something didn't soon break loose, we were going to be in even worse trouble than we already were, but I remained strangely unalarmed about the situation, to the extent that I never bothered to mention it, not even to Joyce. I didn't feel the need to pray about it, although I didn't really understand why. It simply didn't occur to me to address this situation in prayer. I had a confidence that the problem would be resolved, and I just didn't worry.

One evening Joyce showed up at my house unexpectedly with a grocery bag in her arms, asking how things were going with our finances. Her husband and mine had apparently had a long talk earlier in the day, and she wanted to know why I hadn't mentioned that the unemployment check problem had never been solved yet. When she'd heard about this from her husband, she had gone immediately to her freezer, and grabbed a couple of packs of sausage and some homemade bread and coffee, and headed for our house. She said she thought we might be able to use this, and wanted to know what else I needed. I was actually embarrassed, because I felt like a charity case now. I accepted the gift with gratitude, in spite of the embarrassment.

The following day, I was having a real problem with the fact that my sister-in-law had brought food to our house. While I was curling my hair, I was commenting to the Lord on the fact that I was really embarrassed by all this. He answered my comment with, "Do you see the pride?" PRIDE? I asked him what he meant by that. He told me that it was nothing more than pride that was giving me the problem, for although we weren't rich by any means, I had always prided myself on being able to help others, even if it was in a very small way. And now that it was my turn to need help from someone else, it was hurting my pride. Knowing that the Bible says that God hates pride, I quickly renounced it, and the embarrassment disappeared.

Two days later, Sunday morning had arrived, and I was getting ready to walk up to church. I had a little extra time that morning, so I decided to watch a minister on TV until it was time to go. This also seemed like as good a time as any to clean out my purse. While I was cleaning out my wallet, I happened to look into a side pocket, and there was a dollar bill. Wow! I hadn't seen any cash around for weeks, and it was amazing how happy I was to find a dollar. My mind excitedly raced from one thing to another that I could do with this mini-fortune that I had just found. I could get milk, or eggs, or vegetables, or…wait! I suddenly realized that this dollar was of no use to me. I needed too much, and this dollar was too little. The only logical thing I could see to do with this money would be to put it into the church offering, and at least it could be added to everyone else's money, and be put to use that way. With that decision made, I went back to watching the man on TV. This man was a riveting speaker, which caused me to NOT want to turn the TV off when it was time to leave for church, so I opted to stay home and listen to whatever else he had to say. I slipped the dollar back into it's hiding place, and silently vowed to put it in the church collection plate the following Sunday.

As the minister was making his final point, there was a knock on my door. It was one of the ladies from our Bible study group, who lived on the other side of town. She announced that God had told her this morning that she was to do this, and she stood in front of me with her clenched hand held out to mine. "Take this," she said. I was confused by her behavior, but she insisted "Here, take this!" I held out my hand, and she transferred what seemed like a dollar bill into it, and closed my fingers around it.

When I asked her what she was doing, she explained that the Lord had told her this morning to give this to me. She said she had planned on getting a card, and sending it to me, but He had insisted that she not bother with all that, and that she was to bring it to me herself, and she was to bring it NOW. She then said that she had questioned Him, saying that I surely wouldn't be home now anyway, because I never missed church on Sunday mornings. "Now," He had repeated, so she had hopped into her car and driven down to my house, surprised to find me home. That said, she hugged me, and abruptly left, saying something about having to be somewhere else. It wasn't until after she'd left that I opened up that scrunched bill, and saw that it was fifty dollars!

I saw now why God had needed to deal with me about pride a couple of days earlier. If I'd had a major problem with sausage and bread, I knew I would have had an even BIGGER problem with someone bringing me fifty dollars. But the day wasn't over yet.

Later that day, I received a phone call from a lady who refused to identify herself, although I asked twice who it was that was calling. She kept asking me if I were going to be home in about a half-hour, and I finally said yes, wondering if I should have even answered this woman. When I answered her question, she said "

Great! Someone will be at your house in a half-hour!" and hung up. This wasn't making any sense.

About a half-hour later, there was a knock on my kitchen door. I answered it, surprised to find a man standing there with a very large box full of groceries in his hands. He introduced himself, but he didn't need to. I recognized him. This was the same man that I had sent the anonymous card to over a year ago. The only thing he said after he introduced himself was "The Lord told me you needed this. Is there somewhere that I can set it down?" I stepped aside so he could set it on top of the empty freezer sitting inside the door, and he swiftly turned to leave, saying " Don't shut the door...I'll be right back." Completely shocked by this turn of events, I just stood there looking at the box perched on the freezer. I just couldn't believe this!

By the time this man was finished, he had brought five large boxes full of groceries into my house. When the last box had been set down, he grinned from ear to ear, saying "We never have to worry about anything. God provides.", and then he left. How well I could SEE that, AND in the most fascinating ways. I didn't tell that man about the card. I never saw him again. I heard a short time later that he had moved away, but not before God used him to show me how well He's able to connect us all to help one another, whenever help is needed.

The following day, we received one more phone call, this time informing my husband that they had tracked down the problem with the unemployment checks, and he was reimbursed the entire amount that was owed. Everything got paid, and life went back to normal, but not before I got a chance to see God's hand move in a difficult situation. You know, sometimes what seems like our worst times are actually our best times, just waiting to happen.

chapter 21
BLESS THOSE WHO DENT YOU

We come to expect, as children of God, to be misunderstood by the people who've had no spiritual experience whatsoever, for they can't "see" what we've seen. Their blinders have not yet been removed. One of the problems I've encountered, though, that I've found to be MUCH more devastating, is when another Christian accuses you, judges you wrongly to others, or embarrasses you to tears. I've had that type of knife plunged into my heart more than once, and that knife went in deep, because my guard was down, and I was trusting.

I had gone to God in prayer on one of these very occasions, shattered this time, because of the shock of what someone had said about me to others. "WHY, Lord? What did I do wrong? Did I do something to deserve this?" Immediately, I planned to find out from the Lord what I had done wrong to bring this on myself. If I had made a mistake, I wanted to know what it was, so I wouldn't make it again. As I stayed in prayer, the Lord spoke to me and assured me that I was NOT guilty of what had been spoken. Well then, I had asked, why had this woman said this about me? As I continued on in prayer, wanting to know how she even had come up with this story, the word "gossip" appeared in the air, then faded away.

I continued on in prayer until I had gotten a picture as to how this had been able to happen. I came to understand that, had the lady gone to God about what she heard in gossip, He could have stilled her fears. What I saw also was that I could have enlightened her myself, had she asked me about it, but she had judged me instead, because of what she'd heard, so it turned out that SHE was the one who had made the mistake, not me. I was so relieved to know that I wasn't guilty of anything, and that it had just been gossip that had created this. What I didn't know yet, was that I had now come to a pivotal point in the situation. What was I going to do with this information?

Have you ever been so hurt by another Christian that you had trouble recovering from it? Have you not understood how someone who now belongs to God could do these things to you? The problem with me was that I was naïve enough not to understand ahead of time that we're just all new kids learning how to walk. We've already been wrongly taught by the world, and we need to understand ahead of time, that we're dealing with all the fears and phobias that this world has programmed into everyone of us. If we know that ahead of time, we won't be caught off-guard so easily. It isn't this innocent child of God who is speaking against you, but a fear or a wrong teaching that has raised up from within them, that they have not yet conquered. We all need to be rid of the fears in us that will so readily grab hold of gossip. I didn't know that then, so I began to feel indignant that I had been treated unfairly. My natural, reflex-action thought was to never have anything to do with this woman again. She had lied about me to others, and that was totally unfair.

Just then, God broke into my already-forming, religiously-huffy attitude, with one statement. "Bless them that curse you," He reminded me. I wasn't happy to hear this, because I was angry, and I had every right to be! But, I also knew by now that, although I may have to wrestle with this, I'd also have to do it His way. So I finished the prayer with a statement in English, saying "I'm angry, Lord, but bless her, anyway."

This, I came to find out that day, was just not going to be good enough, because God spoke to me again, and said "Read the scriptures concerning this. I got my Bible Concordance out and looked up the KJV references for anything on 'bless them that curse thee', and I found in Matthew 5, "Bless them that curse you". Then in Luke 6, it said the same thing. Romans 12 was next, with "Bless them which persecute you". As I was looking these up in my Bible and going over them again, I started to see something in those scriptures that I hadn't noticed before. The Bible wasn't saying to ask GOD to bless these people. It was saying that I was to bless them MYSELF. Well! This was an eye-opener! It became perfectly clear that I wasn't going to be able to lay this responsibility on God, but I was going to have to bless this woman with whatever it was she needed.. Then another part of those scriptures came to mind, that's in Luke 6, which says, "...and pray for them which despitefully use you.." By the time God and I were done working on the situation that day, this is what all I had learned.

If someone wrongfully uses or accuses you, it only means that there is some light (truth) that they're lacking within themselves that caused them to step on you along their way. PRAY for them. YOU have an unction with the Father. HE knows what they need. They NEED someone to love them enough to go to the Father on their behalf. THEY don't know they need anything, so they would go on in that darkness, continuing to step on people in that area. Go to God, get hold of the light that they need, and pray that light right to them, so they don't have to stumble any more, but will come into that light with you and continue on as sister, or brother, and friend. Don't let hurt pride stand in the way of you helping another out of that darkness. Remember, when you were in darkness, someone prayed for YOU.

I began to pray good things for the lady who had hurt me. I asked for God's light to enter her life in a greater way. Remembering that Jesus had said that anything we asked , in His name, it would be done by the Father in Heaven, I began directing specific things her way in prayer. These were things like prosperity, and health, a healed heart, and on and on I prayed. I sent these things to her myself, in prayer, in the name of Jesus, and from that moment on, instead of thinking of her angrily, I watched her anxiously, waiting to see what great things God would do for her, because I prayed. I felt as though I had sent her a wonderful package in the mail, full of all good things, and my spirit was lifted to a higher place. Not only was I not hurting or angry any more, but I was full of LIFE. You get back what you give out. I gave life and I got life.

I've come to look at all of us battered little children in a new light, and understand that misunderstandings between us are not really as serious as they seem, for they are bound to happen until we get the garbage of this world all out of us, and they can be so easily fixed.

Whatever spirit that we travel in, is sometimes referred to as our vehicle. A lot of us, like myself, come to God because we've been "totaled". We've been wrecked so many times already, that we just can't go any more. When we ask the Lord to take over, He gives us a brand NEW vehicle. We now have HIS Spirit to travel in. What we don't realize yet, is that we were wrecked before because we didn't know how to drive, and guess what? We still don't. And worse yet, neither do any of these OTHER new kids in the Kingdom. Not at first, anyway. We start again, brand new, but with all the more we know about what we're doing, we're like children lining up for the local bumper-car ride, and we can't wait to get onto the racetrack. Is it any wonder that we get bumped and bruised and dented along the way?

We haven't yet learned how to navigate this new vehicle, but we HAVE to navigate it in order to learn to operate it properly. The longer we practice, the better we'll get. But in the meantime, we're in for some jolts. Before we can allow ourselves to get too self-righteously indignant about the dents we're receiving, though, we need to understand that we may just have inflicted a few dents ourselves, in our childlike excitement. It's always good to know that every trip around the track, we can stop and take time with our Father who gave us this new vehicle, to receive more operating instructions, and have the dents we've acquired, repaired. If we learn to continue to stop for repair, (otherwise pronounced "prayer") when the race is over, our spirit (our vehicle) is bright and shining, and undamaged. The secret to finishing this race successfully is in the pit stops!

There are times, however, when we will encounter people who, although they've given their lives to God and have received His Spirit to travel in, they are still driving "under the influence" of things that haven't yet been dealt with It's one thing to receive a few dents from inexperienced drivers, and quite another to receive numerous near-killer crashes from totally self-willed drivers. We're taught to "Drive Defensively" on the highway. Common sense says we need to learn to practice defensive driving on our spiritual path, too.

chapter 22
IS FORGIVENESS ENOUGH?

My house was always known as a gathering place. Everyone knew that they could stop in any time they needed to talk. If there was one thing I'd always take time for, it was prayer with someone who had a question or a problem, and sometimes it was me who had the question or problem, and I was glad someone had come to pray with me.

On one particular afternoon a girl stopped to see if I would pray with her about a forgiveness problem. She said that she had forgiven a close family member over and over again concerning a betrayal that had taken place some time ago, but no matter how many times she forgave the incident, she couldn't seem to get over it. She wanted to be free of this, and she knew forgiveness was the answer, but it didn't seem to be working. She was still carrying the pain as though it had just happened, and she said it seemed to be effecting her life in other ways. She found herself getting more and more depressed over this, and although she kept forgiving, she knew she was getting worse. Together, we took the problem to the Lord.

As we prayed, asking God what was keeping her trapped in the pain of betrayal no matter how much she tried to forgive, He showed me the whole scene of the betrayal in a different way. I watched her walking on a sidewalk, while her trusted family member was approaching on the same sidewalk, from the opposite direction. When they met one another, they both stopped and embraced with a warm, welcoming hug. During the embrace, however, the trusted family member plunged a very large knife deep into the back of this girl, then pulled out the knife, and went on her way as though nothing had happened.

I saw the wide-eyed astonishment on the face of the wounded girl as she turned to watch her trusted assailant walking away. A great deal of blood was pouring from the stab-wound in her back, and as she watched her trusted family member departing, with tears in her eyes, she said, "I forgive you".

The blood kept pouring from the wound, and it was becoming obvious in this vision that she was getting weaker, but still she continued to watch her once-trusted betrayer walking even further away, while she said, more softly this time, "I forgive you." She continued her declaration of forgiveness, while blood continued to escape from the wound. Finally, weakened from the loss of blood, she sank to the sidewalk into a sitting position and, in a whisper this time, she repeated, "I forgive you".

It was easy to see now what was causing the problem. It wasn't that she wasn't forgiving, for she truly loved the family member, and her forgiveness had been sincere. The problem was the wound itself, which hadn't been healed, and the more time that was passing, the weaker she was becoming. She was losing life because of the wound, and we prayed now for the wound to be healed, and for the life that she had been losing because of it, to be restored.

All along, she had felt that she wasn't truly forgiving the one who had hurt her, and that's why she had asked for prayer, but as it turned out, she had done what was needed in all sincerity, but never realized the need to have the wound itself cleaned and closed. If we leave a wound unattended long enough, it can weaken us severely, but worse yet, an infection will set in to an untended wound. This is what too often happens when we have received a physical wound. The same applies to emotional and spiritual wounds. The infection that sets in to an open emotional or spiritual wound, left unattended, is resentment, which turns to bitterness, and eventually drains the spiritual life. We need to forgive when we're wounded, but we must not neglect the healing of the wound itself. Wounds that have seemingly healed through time can hold infection that we're not aware of until we're opened up and examined. It's only then that the wound can be cleaned out properly, and permitted to heal completely.

Sometimes when we have a severe reaction to something someone says or does, we may find that that was nothing more than God causing someone to open up an old wound, so He can heal it from the inside out. You've probably heard the phrase before "If you have a cancer in your life, cut it out." When I heard that phrase, knowing that doctors use scalpels to open up a person to remove cancer, I asked the Lord what HE used to open up a person to remove an infected area in their spirit. His answer was simple. "A cutting remark." When I thought about this, I realized that if someone made a cutting remark to me, and I felt the stab of it, it would be foolish to become angry at the person who had made the remark. After all, hadn't God allowed this for His purpose? Instead of becoming angry, all I needed to do was go to the Lord to find out what it was in me that He was looking for. Once I'd see what the problem was in me, such as a negative attitude, caused by bitterness about something that happened long ago, I'd let Him heal it, and be done with it forever.

We draw those cutting remarks to us by the negatives of bitterness and resentment in us, that old wounds have caused. Otherwise, the remark would not have been felt. It would just have been powerless words. When we feel the pain of a cutting remark, it's because the remark has cut into us to expose something hidden in us, that God knows will cause even worse problems, if not removed. As soon as we feel the stab of a cutting remark, we need to go to the Lord, the great Physician, and allow Him to remove the hidden cancer that drew His scalpel in the first place. Doesn't it make more sense to let Him heal you, than to allow the spiritual cancer to remain, that will kill you?

chapter 23
OKAY...WHO SPILLED THE OIL?

When God is in your life, you can be assured that strange and interesting things are going to happen. He IS a supernatural God, after all. I've seen people raise their eyebrows when the word "supernatural" is mentioned, but keep in mind "supernatural" simply means " above or beyond what is natural".

What we see around us is the natural world. The God we come to know is the same God who parted the Red Sea. Do you suppose that the parting of the Red Sea might have been just a little beyond what the people were used to? Well, God hasn't changed a bit. He's not restricted to our physical laws NOW, any more than He was back then, although I've met many people who seem to believe that He is. I've seen enough by now to know that He's anything BUT restricted! The only thing that can restrict Him in demonstrating His supernatural abilities is our own limited belief systems. While we were still living in that old house, and Bible studies and prayer meetings were practically an everyday occurrence, I saw many examples of His supernatural ability, but for now I'll tell you about just one. Actually, I didn't have any idea WHAT was going on at the time it happened.

I had been on one of my "cleaning streaks", as I called it, all day long. I was scrubbing and polishing and washing and rearranging. These times were a real getting-into-the-corners kind of cleaning, rather than the usual once-over that you can get away with for just so long. This time, it was the kitchen that was under attack. My husband had gone to bed around eleven o'clock, and I had stayed up to add the finishing touches to the kitchen before I could rest. It was probably two o'clock in the morning before I finally had everything done to my satisfaction. The only thing left to do was wax the floor.

I'd been at this room all day, and I was beginning to feel weary, so I opted for one slightly heavier coat of wax this time, rather than take the time to wax, then wait, then wax again. I ran water for a bubble bath while I applied the wax. The bubble bath was my reward for a finished project. It was also my remedy for the aching muscles that were now making themselves known to me. I'd been going strong all day, and now it was time to unwind.

I sank slowly into that bath, grateful for the oh-so warm water that now enveloped my weary body. I was deliciously tired. Deliciously tired is the tired that you feel when you know you've done a really good job, and you relish the thought of waking up in the morning to the results of all your labor. Once the bath was finished, I slid into bed, expecting I'd be up bright and early to put the table and chairs back on my freshly waxed floor. Instead, I slept so soundly that I never even heard my husband get up in the morning. I was usually the first one up, but that morning I never regained consciousness until an hour after the coffee had already been made. When I DID finally start to stir, my husband immediately brought me coffee in bed. Wow, I thought, even HE must be impressed with all that I had accomplished the day before.

Thinking that I was being rewarded for a job well done, I happily took the coffee and took a sip, enjoying the fact that I didn't even have to get out of bed for this. As it turned out, the coffee wasn't a reward, so much as a prompt to assure that I would be fully awake to hear his report. He had been waiting for me to wake up so he could alert me to a problem in the kitchen.

"How much doggone wax did you put on that floor last night?" he wanted to know. "I nearly killed myself out there this morning."

Now, this was hardly the praise I'd been expecting. "What do you mean, how much wax did I put on the floor?" I'm sure my confused state was evident in the tone of my voice. What kind of question was this to start the day?

He repeated, "I could have killed myself out there this morning! How much wax did you PUT on that floor?" Now it was sounding more like an accusation.

I frowned. I was a little irritated by this negative intrusion on the first moments of my day. "What are you TALKING about?" I asked.

While I sipped my coffee, he proceeded to tell me what had happened in the kitchen that morning. He said that he had gone out to make the coffee, and that he had stepped on a spot on the kitchen floor that was so slippery, he had nearly fallen headlong into the cupboards.

Still proud of the job I had done the night before, I hid a faint smile behind my cup. "Wow", I thought, "that's good wax!"

"It's not funny, Vic," I guess I hadn't hidden the smile well enough. He continued, "You'd better get out there and do something about that floor, before someone gets hurt."

Realizing that my morning quiet time wasn't going to happen this morning, I decided I'd better get up and go see what all the fuss was about. I followed Tony into the kitchen, where he promptly reenacted the incident for me. I couldn't see anything on the spot that he had designated as the death trap, but as he talked, I noticed another place on the floor where he had obviously spilled water. There was a good sized puddle just a couple of feet from where he said he'd had the problem, and as I looked beyond THAT, there was another puddle! NOW I was getting angry. There's nothing that will ruin a perfectly waxed floor any faster than water spills that have been left to do their damage. I had been up half the night finishing this kitchen, and now look at this floor!

When I asked him why he hadn't wiped up the water he'd spilled, he said he hadn't even been on that side of the kitchen, so he couldn't have done that. It was hard to believe that he hadn't spilled water though, because there it was, and he'd been the only one out here this morning. As I grabbed some paper towels to wipe up the spills, there was a knock on the door. We both yelled "Come in!", and I went straight to work on that floor. One of my friends had stopped by to bum a cup of coffee after running some early morning errands. I told my friend, as she entered the kitchen, to be careful where she stepped because of puddles on the floor. I didn't want to have to pick her up off the linoleum.

When she asked what was going on, I told her that Tony had apparently spilled water on the floor, and he informed her that he had done no such thing.

The more I wiped up puddles, the more I found. These were not just little water spots, either. They were puddles. Interestingly enough, these water puddles hadn't seemed to dull the wax. It was my friend who noticed that there was a puddle on a countertop, too. She put her fingers into it, and as she rubbed her fingers together, examining this liquid, she said "This isn't water, Vicki, it's some kind of OIL".

Now we all dipped our fingers into the puddle on the countertop, to check it out. Yep, it was oil! Oh, No! Oil WOULD make the floor slippery, because of the residue it leaves behind. But there were no telltale traces of oil on the floor where I had wiped it up. We began checking countertops. Two had oil puddles, as did the stovetop, and the freezer on another wall. I wiped these up too, and again, there was no trace of any oily substance left behind. It was as though nothing had been there at all. All in all, about one third of the kitchen had had oil puddles splattered all over it. This was just too strange.

The three of us now needed to find where this oil had come from. We checked every cupboard, inside and out, and found nothing. There seemed to be no reasonable explanation for the oil, unless it had come out of the ceiling, which we also examined thoroughly. Since the house had been locked up for the night, there was no way that anyone could have entered and done this. The part that puzzled us all the most was that, when you wiped up the oil, it left no trace behind. None of us knew of any oil that didn't leave an oily residue as proof of where it had been.

Once we had exhausted every possible avenue of investigation, there was nothing left to do but go ahead and have our coffee, and begin the day. My friend and I decided that the only way that the oil could have been introduced into my kitchen, would have been to drop right out of the air, which only made us laugh at the thought. It was puzzling, for sure, but there was nothing more we could do. My friend, being a very spiritual person, said that the only other thing she could imagine was that God had anointed the house with oil. We laughed again, for who ever heard of such a thing!

My husband, for lack of any other way to explain the oil, had decided that I must have made popcorn after he'd gone to bed, and spilled oil all over that part of the kitchen, and left it there. Give me a break! We dropped the subject, and continued on with the morning.

A few days later I had to be somewhere early in the morning, and I wouldn't be back until mid-afternoon. Tony had a project going on in his little workshop behind the house, so he saw me off at the front door, before he headed out back to get to work. Nothing more had been mentioned about the oil, I guess because nobody really knew WHAT to say about it. I returned that afternoon to find Tony anxiously awaiting my arrival. He practically ran into the kitchen the moment I opened the door.

"It happened again!" he exclaimed.

"WHAT happened again?" I answered, thinking that if I were a mind reader, I'd have an easier time figuring out what he was EVER talking about.

"The oil! It happened again!" he seemed almost frantic.

Glancing quickly around the kitchen, and seeing nothing, I sat down at the table, and waited for him to explain. In the next few minutes he told me that he had locked the front door after me when I left, since no one would be using it, and headed out the back door to his project. He'd been out there all morning, and when he came in around noon to grab a sandwich, he'd found oil puddles all over the kitchen again, only this time, he said, there were more than before. This time they were here and there, in every part of the kitchen. He had ritualistically checked everything again, once he'd wiped up all the oil, and still could find no reason why it should be here. Again, when it had been wiped up, it left no evidence behind. He was badly shaken by this strange event, because he knew it hadn't been there in the morning, and now he couldn't blame it on me, since I hadn't even been home. This time it had happened with no one in the house, let alone in the kitchen. The man became a believer in the supernatural THAT day.

We started looking for oil every time we went into the kitchen. For weeks I found myself walking around the kitchen every morning and evening, just checking, but finding nothing. If we went anywhere away from the house, we checked everything when we returned, just to make sure. We never saw the oil in the house again.

Weeks later, a friend of mine from another town stopped by one afternoon, which was always a treat for me. In my estimation, there wasn't anything about the Bible that she didn't know. She also kept up with every move of the Holy Spirit by keeping track of what every minister was teaching at all times, as much as possible. Her life revolved around what God was doing. While we visited that day, the story of the oil came up. She listened intently, her head down, while she peered up over the top of her glasses in her comical librarian style. She asked what God had said about it, and I told her that He hadn't said anything. The truth was, I hadn't really ever sat down and asked about it, although the question had always remained in my mind. I had just accepted it as something that had happened. I told her how my other friend and I had joked about God anointing the house, and how we had laughed about that, because, after all, God anoints PEOPLE, not houses.

"Are you aware of the fact that God can anoint ANYTHING?" she peered over those glasses and directly into my eyes.

"Really?" I said, feeling just a little un-informed.

"Oh Dear," she continued, "He can anoint ANYTHING he plans to use! He's not restricted to just people. It looks like God gave you a physical sign of the anointing He has placed on this house for the meetings that take place here." Somewhere deep inside I knew that what she had just said was true, and I accepted her explanation as God's answer to my mental question, as though He Himself had just spoken, and although I never talked about it much to others, I always knew. So much prayer, and so many healings took place in that old house back then, that only the anointing of God could possibly have caused it. A few years later that old house was sold for a phenomenal amount, and believe me, it was only God that caused that, too.

chapter 24
HAPPY LITTLE GO-FERS

Once my husband was off to work each day, I would automatically move into my morning routine. This consisted of reading a few chapters of my Bible, or a chapter of the latest spiritual book that I was devouring, while nursing my morning coffee. One weekday morning, while relishing this ritual, I was startled by a line of scripture that literally invaded my mind, and superimposed itself over what I was reading.

You've heard the phrase "in one ear and out the other", haven't you? Well, these words had just entered the right side of my mind, swooped through at a perfect reading speed, and left again, as if through my left temple, much like a ticker-tape would do. The line, from I Corinth 14:15 (KJV) " I will pray with the Spirit, and I will pray with the understanding also; I will sing with the Spirit and I will sing with the understanding also," was very familiar to me. I had read it so many times.

This intrusion snapped my head up to attention, but I had been engrossed in what I was reading, so I didn't appreciate the disturbance. I shook my head to clear my mind, as one would at any interrupting thought, and went back to reading my book.

A minute later, the intrusion came again. Same words, same way. I pushed it aside again, determining to concentrate harder on the pages of my book. When it happened the third time, I sat straight up in my chair. I had become impatient with this intrusion by now, so much so, that I addressed the situation verbally. "For crying out loud, stop this!"

I spoke sharply to whatever was doing this to me. "C'mon, Lord, help me out here. I want to READ this!" I had now appealed to the Lord for help, in a somewhat fast-food type of prayer, hoping that He had a divine flyswatter handy, and that he would use it on this pesky irritant. After all, I reasoned, this IS a Christian book, and it could only be an enemy of my learning that was pestering me, right? I released a very indignant breath, and with even more determination than ever to complete what I had started, I returned again, for the last time, to my book.

When the Scripture invaded for the fourth time, it's very persistence snapped me out of my self-determined stupor. Suddenly and completely now, I got the point. I felt like a daydreaming school student who has just been addressed by the teacher for the fourth time in front of the whole class. Not daring to look up, I sheepishly closed the book, pushed it aside, and ventured "Yes, Lord? You were saying something?"

Immediately the words came again, only this time I was paying attention. As soon as the words "I will pray with the Spirit and I will pray with the understanding also, and I will sing with the Spirit and I will sing with the understanding also." came, I responded humbly with "Yes, Lord…and?" Then I waited for whatever point was to be made. But what He said to me puzzled me a bit, for He continued with "It wasn't written the other way around".

"Yes Lord, I know." was all I could say, still waiting to get to the point.

"I SAID" He went on gently, but firmly, "it wasn't written the other way around." He spoke this with a great, finalizing authority.

"YES, Lord, I KNOW. I've read it so many times." I felt like He was implying that I may have read it backwards, and I knew I hadn't. "So, Lord, what exactly IS the point here? You must have brought this up for a reason." I was intrigued by now, so I waited, expecting Him to respond with the rest of the story, but the rest of the story never came…not that day, anyway.

I become frustrated with movies that put you right on the edge of your seat, only to stun you with "to be continued", and this brief encounter with the Lord had left me somewhat stunned, also. I waited for about fifteen minutes for a response, before I realized that what He had spoken was all He was going to say. The Scripture remained with me for the rest of the day, as I puzzled over why He had brought it up.

When my daughter had left home to attend business school, I had adopted her room as my sanctuary. It was my hiding place away from the rest of the world. This compact room became my classroom. I had set up my tape player in there, and had a variety of tapes on different subjects that I would listen to every time I got the chance. It isn't that I hadn't heard them all before, but I had learned to go back periodically and listen to them again, just to see what I had missed. I had discovered that, because of the time spent in prayer, and the light that I would receive from God during these times of communion with Him, I could go back to things previously studied, and see so much more than I had seen before.

There is an almost magical mystery about God's truth. It is so simple, and yet so intricate. His truths are revealed to us in layers, according to the light that we carry inside. The more light we receive directly from Him, the more we're able to digest His truths in a more profound and applicable way. It's like walking down a path in the dark with a weak flashlight, then returning to the path with a floodlight. It's amazing how much more you see now, and it's the same path.

It was in this private little sanctuary, the following day, that God would begin to expand on what He had brought to my attention the day before. Prayer! Our Bible study-prayer group had been in operation for a couple of years by now, and we were meeting weekly now at Joyce's. We were doing alright in prayer in the light that we had, but now God had decided it was time for us to move from grade school to high school in this particular subject.

I had straightened the house, and was waiting for a load of laundry to dry, when I decided to take advantage of that waiting time, and listen to a tape. As the man who had made the tape began to teach, I lay on my daughter's bed, looking at the ceiling as though it were a blank screen, while the teacher painted a mental image for me.

I relaxed into the tape, looking forward to what new thing I would come to understand today, some detail about faith that had been previously obscured. I was only about ten minutes into the teaching when I was interrupted by something that caught my eye up by the ceiling, in the air. I glanced momentarily to see what had interrupted my concentration, and was instantly horrified by what I saw. I immediately recoiled my gaze, much in the same reactive way that you would pull your hand away from a hot pan that you've just touched, without realizing it had just come out of a very hot oven.

"OH, LORD! What IS that? "the words came flying out of my mouth as though the sheer force of speed with which I had turned my face away, had catapulted them. What a repulsive sight to find in the air, nearly directly over my head! It had instantly frightened me. "Oh, Lord!" I repeated, "What IS that?"

What I had gotten a glimpse of was a body, dangling in the air, looking as though it were in an alarming state of convulsions. Although I had turned away too quickly to fully grasp the details, I had seen enough to know that it was a gruesome sight. I had no desire to look again.

If I thought that I had been shocked by what I had seen, it wasn't going to compare to the shock of what the Lord was going to say next, after I asked Him "What IS that?" He softly, but solemnly replied, "That IS my body".

"Oh Lord!" I begged to differ with this statement, "It CAN'T be. I know what Your body is, and that's Your children, so that CAN'T be Your body. That body's a mess!"

"Unfortunately," He said sadly "that IS the condition of my body."

"LORD," I insisted, "that can't BE!"

He spoke again. "Notice the head."

I didn't want to look at this vision again, but I wasn't going to refuse to do what He told me, either. Resigning myself to the inevitable, I turned my head again to look at what had repulsed me. The body was there, and still appearing to be in a convulsive state, which I tried to avoid looking at directly. He had said to notice the head, so that's the part I turned my attention to. I looked, but now I noticed that it wasn't the head that seemed to be having the problem. The head of this body appeared to be stable. I realized now that it was just everything attached to the body that couldn't seem to get itself together.

The fear began to subside, so I studied more closely.

"Lord," I said," there doesn't seem to be anything wrong with the head. It's just the rest of the body that's all messed up. So why did You want me to look at the head, when that's not the messed-up part?"

"Who's the Head?" was spoken so quietly in the spirit that, had I not been listening intently, I think I would have missed it. Of course! Why hadn't I thought of that earlier? Christ IS the head of His body, the Bible says so. I was a little slow again today on picking up the message.

"Of course the head isn't messed up, Lord, it's You! Sorry. But Lord, why does the body look like that? I don't understand what you're showing me."

"You understand how the human body functions?" He asked me, and I seemed to understand what He was looking for.

"Yes, Lord," I answered "the body gets its instructions from the brain."

"That's right," he said, then proceeded to usher in another vision for me to watch while He continued to explain. This vision was of a man , bandaged from head to toe, and lying in a hospital bed. The only thing that was moving was his eyes. The Lord then asked me if I understood that a disconnection between the brain and the body would render the body either partially or fully dysfunctional, in spite of the fact that that brain was in perfect condition. A brilliant mind could be sending out instructions all day long, but if those signals weren't being received because of the disconnection, that body would continue to be useless. Even if some messages could come through, without the full connection of the body to the brain, there could be nothing to hope for but a crippled life, much less a fully functional and completely successful one. Yes, I understood.

Then He eased the focus of the discussion over into the comparison with His body. He said yes, we were all parts of His body, but if we weren't connecting with Him, in other words His Mind, we weren't functioning to full capacity, either.

"Each one of you has his own mind, but it is in MY mind that you will find my plan for you, and for every situation. You simply need to connect."

"But how do we connect, Lord? What do you mean?" I wanted to know it all.

"Up until now, you've prayed my perfect will on occasion, but only by accident. At other times you've prayed YOUR will for situations." He said this kindly, not at all condemning. "I am going to show you now how to pray MY will at all times, and then you'll see the difference. Your prayers have not been wrong, for they've been for good, but I see things that are hidden to you, and I will show you how to get to the heart of a problem, and together we will get the job done. You see the tree, but I see the roots. You see the things going on in this world, and you pray about them, and you wonder why these problems return. You see what happens, but I see what caused it. I will show you what I see and where the problem really lies, and we will fix it there, right at the root." I was developing a peaceful anticipation about this, but my question still hadn't been answered.

"But how do we connect with your mind, Lord, to be able to see what you see?"

"I have given you a gift, in the person of the Holy Spirit. He speaks to me through you in languages that you don't understand, but He does much more than this. This language is a tool that is meant to be used. The Holy Spirit within you has the ability to break through any barriers that are in your mind, and connect you to my mind, and to all the knowledge that you need on any given subject. From now on when you pray, you will bring the subject of prayer before me, and allow the Holy Spirit to pray until you receive information concerning my will. Only after I've shown you what I want done, will you pray this in your own language, for now you will have been given understanding concerning my will. Now you will be praying MY will, because you remained in My Spirit until you connected with my will. I have much I desire to do, and I will do these things for you when you ask me, but first you must see what they are, or how will you know what to ask?" He finished this lesson by reminding me of the scripture that He had brought to my attention the previous day. "Do you understand now why I said it wasn't written the other way around?"

"Yes Lord, I think I've got it.

I was really looking forward now to the meeting the following evening. I could hardly wait to tell the others what the Lord had told me. We've always had such wonderful times together, because everyone participated. Each person who attended would come with prayer requests, and things that they had learned throughout the week, and everyone was welcome to share whatever they had. You may think that because EVERYONE shared, there would be some kind of noisy confusion going on, but when the Spirit of God is in charge, there is a natural peace and order that occurs. No one was ever "playing church". We were real people with a real relationship with the Lord, and we had real problems to deal with.

We encouraged everyone to bring in their "praise reports" of what God had done for them since we had seen them the previous week, so we all spent our time between meetings watching for what God was doing. We were the derelicts in the eyes of some of the churches, because we met in in-home studies, without an "ordained" pastor presiding, but we were the greatest Christian therapy group around. We may not have had a lot of formality, but we had the Holy Spirit in charge, and that was good enough for us.

I heard someone comment once, that a person didn't need to be afraid to come to those meetings, even if they had gotten away from God for a while, because when you came back, there were no judgments, only love and acceptance, no matter where you'd been or what you'd been doing. I took that as one of the most beautiful descriptions of what God's church is really all about, not putting people into some kind of religious mold, but loving them enough to allow them the freedom to go learn their lessons, and welcome them back, anxious to hear what they had learned, without condemning them for how they learned it.

The following morning I settled into my breakfast of coffee and reading, when suddenly the Lord resumed the conversation from the day before, which made me laugh inside, because it was a whole day later. He began this conversation as though all those hours hadn't passed at all. Wow, I thought, there really IS no such thing as time in the spirit realm.

"For instance," He went on, "since you're sitting at the table now, you could look at it THIS way. If your mind tells your body to go over to the sink now to do the dishes, but your left arm chooses instead to go to the bedroom to dust, and your left leg decides to walk you to the bathroom, while your right arm moves toward the sink, but your right leg starts moving you toward the front door, do you think you'd get the dishes done?"

I burst into laughter while he was telling me this, as the picture of this ridiculous scene formed in my mind. "No Lord, I don't think so."

"Do you see now what I was showing you in the vision of the body?" He brought me back to the first vision of the body in convulsions. It was starting to make sense. That really WAS the body of Christ, with Him as the head, being perfect, and the members all going off in their own directions. Oh, Dear, I thought, we really DO need to connect to His mind for the proper instructions. That was the third and final day of this series of events that He took me through to get this point across. I really couldn't wait to be in the meeting tonight to share THIS information. Tonight would prove to be a very interesting night in prayer, I just knew it.

By the time we gathered around Joyce's table that night, I felt like I would burst with this new information. I explained it all as I had been shown it. When we entered into the prayer time, we followed the instructions, and waited anxiously to see what would happen. One by one, we brought prayer requests before God. The prayer went like this. Father, we bring this situation before You and ask that You show us what You want us to pray concerning it."

Each time a problem was presented to the Lord, and we asked to be shown His will, we would each one enter into his own prayer language, and allow that to flow until someone, or more than one, would begin to see or hear what the problem was, and what was needed. Then we would pray in agreement with GOD'S will, knowing that we'd gotten to the heart of the problem. It was really amazing to all of us just how much God knew about things that we, of course, had never even dreamed of! Not only was the Holy Spirit directing us into the mind of God, but what we were learning about all types of situations, now that we were allowing the Holy Spirit be the teacher completely, without our mental or emotional interference, were things that no one else could have known. Prayer took an exciting new direction that night for all of us, but none of us knew that the lesson wasn't over. Now it was time for a test, which we presently flunked.

One of the members of our group wasn't there that evening because of her job. She worked in a factory where they rotated shifts, and this week she had to get some sleep before starting her shift at eleven p.m.. She didn't like the job she had at all, but the bills had to be paid. Although she wasn't able to be with us that evening, she would never be forgotten as the final part of this lesson. She called us in a panic, around ten-thirty, from where her ride was supposed to have picked her up. She said that the girl must have forgotten about her, because she had driven right by her, and now she didn't know how she was going to get to work in the next little town, about ten minutes away. She hadn't been able to reach her brother yet, for his phone had been busy, so she had called us as a last resort, apologizing for interrupting the meeting. We offered to have someone take her to work, but she insisted that her brother would take her once she got hold of him, but said she had needed to call for prayer. She was so afraid she'd be late and lose that job because of it. She'd been sick recently and had already missed enough work. If she lost that job, she'd lose her apartment, never be able to get a car, and on and on. I assured her we would pray.

I went back to the table and explained the situation to the others. Immediately we began to pray for Donna. She had had enough struggle as it was, and she surely didn't need this. I rushed right into this prayer, "Donna needs your help right NOW, Lord. We need a miracle here. Either connect her with her brother for the ride she needs, or turn that other girl around and send her back." We were all praying whatever we could think of to help in the situation, when suddenly the familiar voice of the Lord said to me, quizzically "What are you doing?"

Surprised by His question, I whispered, "Praying for Donna, Lord."

"Do you think that you know, more than I, what she needs?" I paused for a moment on this one, not quite understanding where we were going with this.

He continued, "You've done so well this evening with what I taught you, until it came to your friend. Now you've decided that you don't need to ask me first? Do you really think you know my will for her?" I felt like SUCH an idiot right then.

I had just been stopped dead in my tracks, and I looked around to see who else had heard this. No one had, of course. Embarrassed, I had to tell the others at the table what I had just been told. Then we ALL looked like kids who've just been caught stealing candy. Uh, oh. We hadn't done it right. "Erase those prayers, Lord, and let's begin again," I started over. "Lord, we bring Donna's situation before You now, and ask that you show us how to pray for her."

"Ask me to connect her now with the new job that I have prepared for her," was all He said. And so we did. We, left to our own good intentions, were asking God to keep her in a place He wanted to take her out of! Who knew? It REALLY pays to go to God first. Donna, by the way, didn't lose her job over that evening, but she did give it up herself soon after, as God connected her with a whole new vision. Not long after that night, Donna enrolled in nursing school. She's a nurse to this day.

After that night, we became what I refer to now as "God's Little Go-fers." People mention problems that touch our spirits, and immediately we go-fer the information from God that's needed, rather than foolishly touch the situation with our own minds. It's amazing how much easier it is to pray for someone, when you don't carry the responsibility for their lives, or for the outcome.

How many times have we prayed for people and then spent so much time worrying that we didn't pray for the right thing, and maybe we should have prayed this instead, or that instead, and we go back and add to the prayer, and put all kinds of amendments and stipulations around it until all we've ended up with is a great big ball of confusion? No wonder people think prayer is so difficult sometimes. And why did God seem to make it even more difficult by wanting us to pray about EVERTHING? When you discover what we've discovered in prayer, it becomes a joy to pray about everything! It's intriguing, for you've entered into a type of conspiracy with the Creator of the Universe, to help people and to fix things that seem impossible to fix. You've entered into true intercession.

chapter 25
DIDN'T I DO THIS IN YOUR NAME?

As much as I loved reading my Bible, there was a particular scripture that I would read that would bother me. Actually, EVERY time I would read it, it would scare me. It was talking about people who would come to the Lord in the end and say, "Lord, Lord, didn't I do this in your name?" And He would answer with, "Get away from me, I never knew you." (My shortened interpretation of Matt. 7, Living Bible). I would read this and cringe, for I didn't know what it meant, and I was so afraid that I'd be one of the people He would say this to. I couldn't imagine anything worse than thinking you were okay with the Lord, only to have Him reject you in the end. I would read that, and worry, then continue to read things that I COULD understand. One day as I read, I came across the passage again, and having the same feeling of dread, I finally began to talk to the Lord concerning my fear.

I wanted to know how you KNOW if you're doing things right or not. Was there any way to tell ahead of time? How would you know that you wouldn't be sent away in the end? What did this scripture mean, I needed to know, so I asked Him directly to explain it to me. He used an unusual illustration to teach me that day, but by the time He was finished, I'd never wonder again. Ronald Reagan was president at the time, so the Lord used him as an example that I could understand.

He began by asking me if I knew who Ronald Reagan was. Surprised by the question, I said "Yes! " Gosh, everybody knew who he was. He said that I was to imagine that even though I'd never actually met him, I had studied everything there was to read about him, to the point that there wasn't anything I didn't know about him. Okay, got that, Lord! Then He said to take it a step further, and imagine that I even knew people that worked for him, and that they had told me everything they ever saw him do. Okay, Lord, got that too! Then He took it even further, by asking me to imagine that I had become personal friends with the members of his family. I was to imagine that I was so close with them, that I had even gone on picnics with them. They included me in some of their family gatherings as though I were family myself, and because they loved to talk about Ron, I had learned a lot of really intimate family secrets about him. Wow, Lord, this is interesting! He said to imagine that, since I knew so much about him, I would spend time with people, talking about the things I knew.

He told me to imagine that because of my extensive knowledge about the president, I just referred to him as "Ron", and neighbors and friends would come to ask me things about him. Then he said to imagine that as neighbors and friends talked to others about how much I knew about the president, others started to come to hear what I had to say. He told me to understand that I had become very satisfied that I was probably the most informed person around, on the subject of Ronald Reagan, and that I took great pride in all of my knowledge.

Then He said that one day a group of these neighbors and friends expressed their heartfelt desire to meet him in person. So you tell them that this is not a problem. You can take them right to the capital yourself, and introduce them! You get a bus, and fill it with these people who are longing to meet the president, and you all laugh and talk and sing songs the entire time of the trip. You smile to yourself, having planned your arrival time, and you've already determined how you're going to surprise Ron with this entire busload of fans. Since you know so much about his habits, and his schedule, you know exactly what time to pull that bus up to a side entrance, because you know that it's his habit to be in this part of the house every day at this time.

You pull the bus out to the side entrance of the White House, and park. You tell the others to wait there while you go and clear the meeting with him. You're bursting with pride at the thought of how pleased these people on the bus are going to be because they're actually going to get to meet the president of the United States, and YOU are the one who gets to introduce them. What a wonderful day!

You're smiling with anticipation as you walk down the sidewalk to the door. You know that Ron will be in this room, and you also know that there won't be anyone else there with him at that time, so you're expecting him to answer the door himself when you knock. You are not disappointed, either. You knock boldly on that side-entrance door, as you look back at the others who are watching expectantly, and you smile a reassuring smile. The door opens, and there you stand, looking right into the face of the one you have studied for so long.

You've learned so much about him, that you greet him like a long-lost friend. You give him your brightest smile, and explain that these people wanted to meet him so badly, so you just got a bus and brought them down. You make a sweeping gesture with your arm, as if to guide his gaze to the excited people waiting on the bus.

He hasn't said a word, and you wonder why he just stands there looking at you. He hasn't even looked at the bus to see that what you're telling him is true. You wonder why he is so silent, never taking his eyes off you. He's been studying your face while you've been talking, and he finally breaks his silence with one statement. "Go away," he says, as he's closing the door. "I've never met you."

Ronald Reagan didn't care how much I knew about him. That wasn't going to get me in the door. The fact was, all my years of study made no impression on this man. Had I met him personally, and gotten to know him, that would have made all the difference, but since I'd spent all my time learning about him, rather than meeting him, and walking and talking with him, the fact remained, I didn't really know him, nor did he know me. Now I stood there frozen, realizing that all my confidant bragging about taking these people to meet the president had been a very foolish thing to do. They had all watched him close the door in my face.

That day I understood what the scripture meant. I breathed a sigh of gratitude to the Lord for hearing me when I said I wished He could make me interested, for had I not met Him, I very well could have fallen into the trap of religion sometime later in my life, where I would read about Him, but never really meet him, and never really talk with Him like I had just done today.

The day came when I had to look a little deeper into what this scripture meant, for I was going to meet a minister who's statement stirred up a question in me that wouldn't go away.

We were all gathered in another lady's house the evening that this minister arrived. He had stopped by to see the owner of the house about something else, and hadn't known that we would be having a meeting there that night. He was invited to join us, and we were thrilled when he said he would. We were pretty crowded in the living room, so there was no place for him to sit. I happily gave up the rocking chair that I'd been occupying, since, being used to crowded gatherings like this, I was equally used to sitting on the floor because of it. I ended up sitting almost at the man's feet. I loved the idea of meeting a minister in relaxed setting like this, because you never knew what kind of experience he had had with the Lord, that he'd be willing to share with the rest of us! He was family, after all, and we couldn't wait to get to know him.

We had been talking about how we had come to know the Lord, and we all had a story to tell about the moment we had met Him. The minister seemed a little withdrawn, compared to the excitement of the others, and I became concerned that he was feeling left out. When there was a pause after someone's glowing report about meeting the Lord for the first time, I thought it an opportune time to draw him into the conversation too, so he would feel more "included". I tilted my head upward toward him, and said, "When did you meet the Lord? How did it happen?"

I can still see his fist come down on the arm of that rocker, as he loudly stated, "You people don't understand anything! I didn't HAVE to have an experience. I was raised in church!"

He seemed angry, and I was so embarrassed. My desire to make this man feel welcomed, had just backfired. I thought for sure I had done something wrong, for this minister to become actually upset with my question. I hadn't meant to upset him, but I thought he would just naturally be as excited as the rest of us about meeting Jesus. Well, I was wrong. The minister left shortly after his outburst. I felt so badly that I had put him on the spot, but worse than that, I was uneasy with what he had said. I had been raised in church too, but that hadn't brought me into a relationship with the Lord. Maybe, I thought, I was just such a hard case that I was the exception, and other people DID know him from being raised in church. His statement bothered me for a long time, until I mentioned the incident to another minister, who had known the Lord for twenty years more than I had, and when I told her just how much that statement had bothered me, she said she understood. She said that she had encountered people, too, who had had the same negative reaction concerning meeting the Lord, and that she had gone to God with the same troubled question. That was the first time I ever heard the statement "I may have been born in a garage, but that doesn't mean I'm a car." Then I understood why I hadn't been able to settle with what the minister had said.

At a later time that scripture became a little more unveiled as I continued to read and study and pray. I was reading the old familiar Adam and Eve account, when I got to the part where Adam "knew" his wife, and they conceived a son. I understood that that word "knew" meant intimate relationship, but as I read it this time, another scripture went through my mind. "Get away from me, I never "knew" you."

Intrigued, I began a study on both those words, and came to find they were the same. When the Lord said "I never knew you", here was more evidence that He values an intimate, personal relationship, or intimate conversation, far more than any amount of work we can do in His name. All of the study on earth about Him is just NOT the same as KNOWING Him.

chapter 26
THE PERFECT SOLUTION.

I had been working at the registration table with a spirit-filled women's group for a few months when I met a woman that I would form a lasting spiritual bond with. She had come into the meeting one morning with some other ladies, and from the moment she walked in the door my attention was drawn to her. Any time I've had that kind of drawing, it's proven to be a stepping-stone relationship. By this, I don't mean a relationship where one person uses another to climb higher. I mean a relationship where two people meet, and walk together for the purpose of both coming to a higher level of understanding.

I felt as though I HAD to get to know her. I didn't know why it seemed so important to me, but it was. It wasn't long before I got the chance to get to know her, because she began coming to the Bible study meetings in my home. We formed a friendship, which was pleasant, but God had an even greater experience in mind for us. It was through my friendship with Virginia that I would come to understand even more about the miracle of "two in agreement" in prayer.

One summer evening I was talking on the phone with Virginia, while my husband was out in the back yard cleaning wood. By cleaning wood, I mean that he was hammering the nails out of used boards that he had gotten, in order to cut and stack the wood that he would burn later as fuel for a wood-burning stove. He came hobbling into the house while Virginia and I were on the phone, and it was easy to see that he was in a great deal of pain. I immediately told Virginia to "hold" as I quickly laid the phone aside and went to see what had happened.

My husband said that he had become distracted by a bee flying around his face while he was hammering the nails, and he had missed a nail and hit his kneecap instead. He was in a excruciating pain, and I said immediately that he needed a doctor. My husband was a stubborn man, not a person to go to doctors easily, so he said "no" and insisted on just going to bed.

Virginia , still on the phone, had heard the conversation in the background, and as soon as I picked the phone back up, I heard "We have to pray!" I agreed, and we quickly took the situation to the Lord to see what was needed. As we prayed in the language of the Spirit, I saw a kneecap with a hairline crack right down the middle. AH! So it was cracked! As we remained in the spirit prayer, I watched the hairline crack seal itself back up in the same way that an open zipper would be drawn back together, from the bottom to the top. By seeing this, I understood the prayer that was needed. We agreed that the crack in the kneecap would close back up again, slowly and carefully, from bottom to top, pinching nothing along the way, and return to normal It was a simple prayer, no emotion involved, and the final instruction I received was to declare that this would be completely healed during the night, and by morning it would be as though nothing had ever happened. When the prayer was finished, we said "Amen", then said our "goodnights" and ended the conversation.

I made a bed on the sofa that night, so I wouldn't disturb Tony, who had appeared to be asleep when I had peeked into the bedroom to check on him. He had only taken a couple of aspirin before he had hobbled off to bed. The following morning, he came out of the bedroom walking normally, and when I asked him how the knee felt, he said it was as though he had never hit it at all! There was no pain whatsoever, and he was thrilled to report this, since he had thought during the night that he would probably have to go in the morning to have it x-rayed. I was so excited that the knee was healed, exactly as we had asked, that I blurted out that we had prayed for that knee to be healed by morning.

I wasn't expecting the anger that my husband displayed when I told him about the prayer. Shouldn't he have been grateful to God for the knee being healed? As it turned out, he was upset about the WAY we had prayed. He said he had tossed and turned most of the night because the throbbing pain in his knee wouldn't allow him to sleep. The pain had begun to subside as morning was approaching, and he had finally drifted off to sleep for a couple of hours. Apparently he was acknowledging the power of prayer, but he was angry that we had agreed that it would be as good as new by morning, and wanted to know why we said "morning", rather than immediately. He felt, in his weary state, that we had deliberately left him to suffer through all that pain for the entire night. When he demanded to know why we said "by morning", all I could tell him was that's the way I was directed to pray. At first I almost felt guilty about that, but that's how I had been directed, so that's the way it was done. I left all thought of guilt behind, and thanked God for the absence of pain and a healed knee.

Virginia and I had many times of our "matter-of-fact" agreements in prayer. By matter-of-fact, I mean calm, without fears and frenzies, just calmly knowing that God has the answer, and waiting for Him to reveal it. Praying that way always brings the same results. Everything takes place as we ask, once we knew the will of God. The way God showed me what happens when we pray that way, is in another picture.

What I saw was that He, already knowing what we're going to need, waits above us with the answer in His hand. It is His perfect answer for the situation. When we come to Him and ask what He has for us, He shows us the perfect answer that He has been waiting to give us. Once we see what He has already prepared, we ask for that, in every detail that He showed us. Then it is so easy for Him to hand it over, since it had already been prepared, and complete. If we ask for something else, something that we THINK is needed, without asking what He's already waiting to give us, He has to lay aside His perfect solution, in order to give us what we asked for, instead. He can give us what we ask for in agreement, but wouldn't we rather have the PERFECT answer?

One prayer solution that I thought was amusing was the time Virginia's company had a deadline to meet, and my husband had actually been sent on that job with their work crew to help meet that deadline. They were working on a building, and my husband, having been a roofer for years, had been recruited to help. We had a lot of threats of rainstorms during that time, which would have stopped the men from working, and since the deadline was near, and many people's jobs were involved, Virginia and I spent mornings in prayer concerning that job. Everything was going well, until one of their best workers had to be taken home with very severe flu symptoms. There was a raging flu going around at the time, and this poor guy had apparently fallen victim to it.

Virginia called that evening to tell me about it, because she was in the habit of praying for their workers, but I'd already heard about this young man's dilemma from my husband when he had gotten home that day. He had talked about how sick that guy had become, and that someone else had had to take him home, because he had become so weak, so quickly, from the illness, that he would never have been able to drive. This flu was keeping people down for a week or two, so we knew we had to pray for him.

This time, the instructions were to address every symptom, and then the cause of those symptoms. We dismissed the fever, body aches, the stomach upset, and anything else the Lord showed us that needed to be removed. Each adverse symptom was replaced with what needed to be in a healthy individual, then we dismissed the root cause. As we finished the prayer, and were about to hang up, I had a very quick "P.S." that I was shown, to add to what had already been prayed for him. I quickly said "Oh, and all the energy that was drained from this young man from the symptoms, we call back to him now, and we call it back doubled, since it was robbed from him in the first place!" Virginia laughed at that, and said "Amen.", and our work was done for the day. The rest was up to God.

The following day when my husband returned from the job, he was completely exhausted. The part of the job that he was doing, he had done in partnership with the man we had prayed for the evening before. When my husband came home drained, I assumed that the guy we prayed for must not have come back to work yet, and Tony must have had to do his part of the job by himself that day. Imagine my surprise when my husband informed me that that had not been the case at all, and if the other guy HADN'T shown up, Tony's day would have probably been much easier! He said not only had the flu victim come to work that morning with no flu symptoms whatsoever, but he'd literally worked circles around my husband, and my husband was completely exhausted from trying to keep UP with his pace all day!

I've learned that if we take the time to go to God on every day matters, each day becomes an adventure in miracles. We need more of those in our lives. It certainly takes the boredom out of every day living, along with that sense of helplessness we sometimes feel, in the face of adverse circumstances. It's much more fun to see what God can do with any little thing, than to just sit back and let negative circumstances rule.

Another amusing prayer time with Virginia comes to mind right now, when she called to tell me that it looked like they would have to cancel the plan for her son's birthday party AGAIN. He wanted to have friends come to their camp for a skiing party. His birthday is in January, and they'd had more than one disappointment when planning this type of party because of a lack of the appropriate amount of snow needed for a day like that.

This time, the ski party was requested and planned again, but the weather wasn't looking like it was going to accommodate this time, either. She really wanted to see what could be done about this weather situation. They needed a lot of snow, in order not to have to cancel the ski party one more time, but my problem with that was that I would be traveling through the same area that weekend, and certainly wasn't going to look forward to bad roads for driving.

We prayed for a while, then I "saw" the solution. We asked for a deluge of snow to provide what was needed for the day for her son and his friends, but that the roads would remain clear for the travelers. I probably don't even have to tell you what happened. We ended up with a blizzard-type pile-up of snow the day before the party, right in the area of the camp. The best part was that the roads never even had to be cleared, for it barely bothered to snow on them that entire weekend

Everyone was safe and happy. There's a solution to meet all needs, no matter how big or how small, when God has put a desire in our hearts. And even when you seem to have opposite desires from your prayer partner's request, that doesn't mean that one person surrenders their need being met for the sake of the other person's situation. A challenging request is not a challenge to God at all. He created the universe. Is there anything in it that He can't fix or control?

A snow weekend may seem like a trivial thing to ask for, but nothing is trivial to God when He Himself has put a desire in the heart of one of His children. He loves to show what He is able to do, and He loves to make us happy. He is a Father, in the truest sense of the word. He will bless us and discipline us, according to what we need. We need to pay attention to the desires in our hearts, for He has put them there. When He puts them there, don't think for a moment that He's not able to fulfill them, for He is well able. I wonder how many blessings we've missed because we've discounted heart-felt desires, thinking that God wouldn't care about some of them. Remember this...He cares about them, for He has authored them. We just need to go to Him with these desires, voice them to Him, and wait for His answer. He moves in answer to the prayers of His people.

When we come to a point where we feel down and discouraged, we need to remember that our Father is a supernatural being, full of supernatural power. He is a God of Miracles, and we need to remember to expect miracles, and allow our Father to show us who He really is. Any lesser expectation would be an insult to His power.

As a parent, wouldn't you love to know that your child believes in your strength and ability to handle situations and solve problems? Wouldn't it hurt you to find out that your child thinks he's all alone in his dilemmas, and thinks that you don't care? Or worse yet, what if your child thinks that you're weak, and unable to help him in any way? Wouldn't you love to have him bring his problems to you, so that you could help him? And wouldn't you love for him to express to you the desires of his heart, so you can show your love by helping to fulfill those desires? Most of all, just knowing that you're trusted in the relationship with your child, and that he wants to share everything with you, is the greatest privilege of all.

God, being a Father, wants the same type of relationship with us. He doesn't want to be shut out of any part of our lives, any more than we want to be shut out of OUR children's lives. He also enjoys being trusted and looked up to, and depended on. He's, after all, a very loving DAD.

chapter 27
PRAYING THROUGH

A minister friend of mine used to say what a difference there was between "praying through", and just "getting through praying". I have to agree. Here's a perfect example.

My mother lived in a town about ninety minutes away from me. One morning I received a phone call, informing me that my mother had been taken to a local hospital. They said she had had a heart attack, and I was already grabbing my clothes to wear to go down there, when my sister-in-law called for our morning prayer time. I told her what had happened, and she immediately said she'd come pick me up, and we'd go together, rather than have me drive down there myself. Besides, she said, we'd be able to pray in the car. I no sooner got into her car, when both prayer languages were engaged. We drove for the hour that it took to get to where the hospital was, and never spoke a word of English. We prayed quietly out loud the entire trip, and when we got to the hospital, we had not yet prayed this through, for the pressure in our spirits hadn't lifted, and we had not yet heard from God on the situation.

I knew I needed to get into that hospital, but I knew I had to hear what God had to say before I went. We parked in the parking lot, and just continued to sit in the car and pray for another fifteen minutes, when suddenly the "tongues" subsided, and God began to speak. "She will not die, but she will live yet years" was all He said.

Satisfied that He had spoken, we entered that hospital assured and calm, while others in her family, who lived closer and had already arrived, were solemnly upset. I'm sure they were not pleased to see that I didn't seem to be disturbed. To the world, it seemed I didn't care. What no one knew was that I had heard from God, and all was well. They were making arrangements to send my mother to Pittsburgh for an emergency angioplasty, wanting to immediately do something about the blockage in the vein that had caused the heart attack. This news set off an alarm system in my spirit, so I told them I would take her myself. I wanted a second opinion before they would put her into surgery.

I don't know medicine, but I DO know when something is not going according to God's plan, because of His subtle, inner alarm system. The Holy Spirit is the Spirit of truth. When He hears a lie, or knows a wrong turn is about to be taken, He is disturbed, and you FEEL it, in the form of an uneasiness deep within. When my mother was able to be released that day, we brought her home to my house. I immediately called a very good doctor in my area, and made an appointment for the following morning. Mom seemed fine for the moment, and after she had eaten some lunch, we stayed at the table and prayed with her.

While we prayed, I watched an interesting scene. Two little monkey-like "culprits" were flitting around her in the spirit. One was hovering around her head, and the other was jumping on her chest. I said nothing, because I didn't want to alarm my mother, but when we finished the prayer, since Mom was tired now from all that had happened, I took her to a bedroom and got her settled for a nap. While she slept, I told Joyce what I had seen. She and I addressed this in prayer, and by the time we were finished, these little culprits were gone.

Next, I received a phone call from the head of cardiology in the hospital in Pittsburgh where my mother was originally to be sent, wanting to know why she wasn't there yet. He had apparently been informed that this was a life or death emergency, and was surprised to hear that she had made the trip to my house just fine, had lunch, and was now taking a nap. He agreed that a second opinion was always a good idea, but expressed his concern that she was still so far away from the hospital. He calmed as we talked. I had noticed that Joyce had gone back to prayer while I was on the phone, but now I was seeing her nearly doubled over in a more travailing prayer. The doctor suddenly asked

"She doesn't have any other problems then, does she?" I told him "No, nothing other than an ulcer, but that's controlled with medication." The surprise in his voice when I told him that she was being treated for an ulcer, let me know that he hadn't been informed of this before.

When he asked what she took for the ulcer, I told him. He asked how long she'd been taking this medication. I told him that she'd been taking it for a couple of years, to my knowledge. There was now dead silence on the other end of the line for about thirty seconds. I didn't know what had happened to the doctor, but when he finally spoke, I sensed in his voice, a controlled anger, as he said " Mrs. Cherry, are you aware of the fact that that medication can have severe side effects, and should never be taken for more than a few weeks?" No, I informed him that I didn't know that, but added that surely her doctor would have been aware of that fact. He said, more firmly now, that a second opinion was a good idea, told me what to tell the new doctor, wished us luck, and gave me his phone number, in case I needed him for anything. I thanked him for the call, and for his concern.

The next morning Mom and I went to the next appointment. Some tests were done, and an x-ray was ordered. The results of the x-ray showed that my mother had an active ulcer that needed immediate attention, and if not dealt with now, could prove to be fatal. The tests also confirmed a slight heart attack. Two different medications were discovered on her list of medications that were doing her more harm than good (two culprits causing trouble?) so they were both removed, and the ulcer medication was replaced with a better one that didn't have the side effects. Her diet was changed, and within a couple of weeks the ulcer was healed, and we could now look into the heart situation.

We went to Pittsburgh now to a different hospital, where she was tested, and the blockage was found, but they felt the angioplasty would not be a safe way to go with her, because of her age. She had had a slight heart attack, but nothing had been damaged because other veins had kicked in to feed the area. The problem with the balloon, they informed me, was that they had no way of knowing how long the blockage had been there, and if it had been there a long time, it would have become brittle. The balloon being inflated could cause a piece to break off, causing an immediate heart attack. Since she was now seventy years old, they saw no need to put her through the danger of it. They chose instead to put her on one pill a day to keep the veins opened up for a better blood flow. She lived another ten years with that pill, and no further ulcer problems, and we had many more good times before she would finally go home to be with the Lord.

The angioplasty, that had been automatically scheduled by people in a panic, could have seriously harmed her, as could the ignored ulcer situation, but these things never happened because God had spoken, and we chose to follow His lead rather than the panic of men. Don't get me wrong. I believe doctors are important. They serve an important purpose but, just like the rest of us, if they're subject to fear and assumption, rather than God, they can make mistakes just as easily as the rest of us. God, on the other hand, never does.

I've found that when we're "praying through", we're simply praying through all the muddled-up thoughts in our own minds, praying past judgments, pre-conceived notions and misconceptions, to get straight to the truth. Sometimes we have to engage the Holy Spirit's power to pray through the force of another person's will for us, that keeps us from following God.

I once had a really frustrating time in prayer that reduced me to tears. I kept seeing an image of myself in a barred cell, like a prison cell. As I would pray, the front wall of the cell would come down slowly and steadily, like a drawbridge being let down. I had been experiencing a lot of inner frustration at the time, as though I couldn't seem to move forward in my spiritual life. I'd had a sense of being trapped somehow, but I hadn't been able to pinpoint the problem, so I was more than happy to see in the spirit, that this wall was coming down. It came all the way down as I prayed, and just as I was ready to step out, the front wall raised back up, and closed in on me again. Startled, I returned to prayer, and watched the front wall come down again. Just as I could have stepped out again, the wall went quickly up again, confining me still to the cell. This happened over and over while I just sat quietly praying in the spirit, and watching. As frustration finally turned to downright anger, I asked the Lord what kept putting the wall of bars back up, so that I couldn't take a step forward! He immediately answered "The prayers of "do-gooders".

These, it turned out, were people who were praying for me things that THEY wanted to see in my life. The Lord said these were prayers based on their ASSUMPTIONS of what I needed, and what was best for me. The words of their prayers had wrapped around me like so many bars of a cell, imprisoning me in such a way that I couldn't move forward on the path that I needed to walk. No wonder I was frustrated! I wanted to call everyone I knew, and just say, "STOP! DON'T pray for me anymore. You're KILLING me!" When I told my prayer partner what I'd seen, and what God had spoken to me, we went to war against this prison. When the two of us prayed together, we not only got the wall down again, but we stayed with this project until that front wall was completely dissolved, and I finally stepped out.

I adopted the habit after that of telling my friends that if they felt the need to pray for me, please just let the Spirit pray, and not to speak a word of English unless God told them what words to speak. We can do more harm than good by praying for others, without God's instruction. Which "will" do you really want for them …yours, or God's? Which one do you want for yourself? Any time I feel like rushing into prayer for another, I have to stop and remember my prison cell. Then I just allow the language of the Holy Spirit to pray for the one who's laying on my heart, knowing full well that He's the only one who really knows what's needed.

chapter 28
EYES OF UNDERSTANDING

Isn't it sad that, when we're blind, we can't see how many people we're stepping on while we grope our way through life? I was no exception. I hurt a lot of people in my blind search for real love, and I wasn't even aware of it. But boy, just let another blind person grope their way across MY path, in that very same search, and accidentally step on ME, and all of a sudden I'm AWARE. I'm aware because I'm feeling a fresh NEW pain, on top of the dull ache I already live in. For instance, my first husband had stepped on me HARD, and how I had howled. No one would hear the end of MY tale of woe.

I'd known the Lord for a couple of years now, was remarried, and I was STILL having a problem forgiving my former husband who had vowed to love me forever, but had chosen to be violent instead. I knew by now that I really needed to forgive him, but I just couldn't bring myself to do it, and mean it. What was holding me back from being able to do that was a lack of understanding. Every time I tried to forgive him, my major life question would get in the way. I kept saying to God, "WHY?". Why did he keep doing those things to hurt me so much? Why did he do these things to ME, when I had loved him?

One day I gave up the battle of trying to do what was right, and simply said, "Lord, I'm just not able to forgive him. I've tried and tried, but I just can't, because I can't forgive what I can't understand. Please give me new eyes to see him. I need to be able to see him as YOU see him, Lord. Then, maybe I could finally forgive him."

As I sat praying in the quiet stillness, I became aware of a subtle movement in front of my face, like a ripple in the air, as though some invisible curtain had just been pulled aside from in front of my eyes. Suddenly it was as though I were standing in the kitchen of the house my ex-husband had grown up in.

I could see through the glass in the kitchen door, and as I watched, I saw a boy between ten and twelve years old coming home from school, his school books in his arms. The boy was my ex-husband at that age. I watched as he entered the house through that kitchen door. He never called to anyone to announce his arrival, for he already knew there was no one there. I watched him put his things away, then go across the street to a neighbor's house. A moment later he emerged from that house, holding the hand of his little sister. I watched as he walked her home, got her settled with something to keep her entertained, then picked up the note that was lying on the kitchen table.

I could see the paper clearly, and on it was a list of the things he was to have done when his mother and step-father got home from work. He read the note, then put it down and proceeded to begin running dishwater for the dishes that had been left in the sink from breakfast. When the dishes were done, he got potatoes out and began to peel them, getting them ready for his mother, all the while keeping a close eye on his younger sister, making sure she was okay. The kitchen was immaculate and attractive, but as I watched the boy in the vision, I felt the emptiness in that house, and the loneliness inside the boy. There'd been no one there to greet him, and as I watched how routinely he performed his chores, I understood that this had become a way of life for him. I realized that he had been, back then, what they now call a "latch key kid", a child who comes home to an empty house every day, because the parent, or parents, are working.

Tears of compassion began to fill my eyes as I realized how much this boy had needed to be hugged and cared for by his parents, rather than him coming home to take care of things for them. I was seeing something that my first husband had never talked about...his childhood. I was looking at the past, and seeing the loneliness in which he had grown up. I wanted to scoop him up and tell him how important he was, and how loved he was, and ask him how his day at school had been, but I couldn't, for that time period that I was watching had long since passed. I was looking at a vision.

As the vision faded, I now understood how empty his life had been, too. He had needed the same things I had. He had needed to feel loved and appreciated, and protected, the same as I had. I was crying now, wishing things had been different for him. I felt a deep compassion for him that I had never felt before. I was not only seeing him through God's eyes of understanding, but I was feeling the same compassion for him that God felt. This whole issue was no longer about ME, and forgiving what he had done to ME. The issue was now about HIM, and what life had done to HIM.

As I cried for him, instead of asking God to help me to forgive him this time, I was asking God to help him to forgive ME for not being able to be the wife that he had needed. How was THAT for a switch! I had spent years not being able to forgive someone, for I could only see through the eyes of my own pain, and in one momentary vision, I witnessed someone else's pain, while all of mine dissolved in a pool of understanding. Now I understood that the things he had done that had hurt me, hadn't been meant to hurt me at all. I knew now that he had been driven by a deeper need, and that was not only to dull the pain he had inside, but also to continue to search for the love that he had not yet found, a love that could take AWAY his pain. It didn't matter now whether he had loved me or not, or whether he had hurt me or not. The only thing that mattered now was the boy who needed to be loved.

I had not been able to give him the stability that he had really needed, for I was entirely too needy myself. I now saw how much of a disappointment that marriage had been for him, too. We had both been searching for the kind of love that heals, although, at the time, neither of us knew that. I had been the lucky one, for I had FOUND that love in the person of Jesus Christ. With one vision, I no longer needed to forgive my first husband ANYTHING, for there was nothing to hold against him. For the first time, I truly understood the title of the song that says "He looked beyond my faults, and saw my need." How can you possibly hold anything against someone who's pain has been revealed to you? Whose innocence has been shown to you? I truly believe that this is the key to being able to "love the sinner, but hate the sin". What God had shown me that day was the child inside the man, and what that child had needed all along, and what I had been unable to give.

The Bible says we're to become like children. Maybe we should all spend more time asking God to show us the children in one another, rather than what those children have had to become to fit into the supposedly grown-up world. We don't need to fix our eyes on what they did to us (or do), as much as we need to see WHY. It would be so much easier that way to live in a forgiving atmosphere. And it's only in a forgiving atmosphere that people are released to heal and to grow.

I've got a feeling that if we spent more time asking to see people through God's eyes, we'd get straight to the heart of a person and see them in their innocence, the same as HE does. Isn't that how we'd like others to see US? As innocent children? Because you know, in our hearts, we are. There's always a child in each one of us who wants to be loved and accepted, acknowledged and praised. Some children HAVE been, and others have not. The ones who have NOT are the ones who display the worst behavior. It isn't because they're evil, but it's because they're angry, and they're angry because they're wounded.

Imagine a world full of emotionally stable, loved, and satisfied children, overlooking one another's mistakes, no matter what age they APPEAR to be. We'd play happily and joyfully together, creating a literal "Heaven on Earth" situation. Do you think it can't be done? How would we know if we never try? I know people would call me an idealist, and I do consider that life like I just described WOULD be ideal, but as children of God, should we so easily settle for anything less? Would HE?

chapter **29**
IT'S ALL ABOUT TIMING!

On occasion, we would fill a car with people from our prayer group, and drive to Ohio to attend a church that was led by a very dear friend, and one of our most enlightening teachers. It was a three-hour drive, so it wasn't something we did all the time, but it was always such an exciting time for those of us who went. We would go halfway, then take an exit off the interstate to get coffee and stretch our legs. We'd finish the trip, sit through church, and head home. We'd get part way again, and have to stop for bathrooms, lunch, and more leg-stretching. We would go out to the church anticipating, and come back filled.

Joyce drove the last time some of us made this trip, which was in the spring of that year. I was glad she was driving this time, because my poor old car had been ailing for a while now, and we weren't sure how much longer it would last. I knew it was time to replace it, and I had decided to look into that when this weekend was over.

Once we returned from that Sunday trip, my husband appointed himself as my constant reminder about my car. Every day for the next two weeks, he told me to get my car up to the dealership and trade it in. As much as I knew I had to do this, I couldn't seem to get past what felt like a giant concrete barrier in my chest. My mind said "Go," but inside me was a reluctance, a holding back, that rendered me unable to budge. After two weeks of my stalling, Tony was getting angry, and I was getting embarrassed that I couldn't move forward on this. It was as though there was an invisible wall in me, concerning that car, that I couldn't break through.

We had already been to the dealership to see what was available in my price range. There were only two cars available right now that I could afford, but that didn't matter. I needed a car, and that was that. They had explained what my car was worth as a trade-in, even with the problems I was having with it, so it all should have been so simple...so why wasn't it? My car, of course, had gotten even worse in these couple of weeks since we'd returned home from Ohio, and I was afraid if I waited much longer, I wouldn't even be able to drive the car across town to make the trade at all.

The car I had was paid for, and I wasn't sure yet how I was going to fit a car payment into my already lean budget, but things like that always had a way of working out, so that wasn't the problem. At the end of that two-week period, I awoke one morning, and felt a release inside The reluctance that had held me back concerning the car was finally gone. Everything fell right into place in my mind, and I was even able now to see how to rearrange the budget to fit in a car payment.

I was excited about trading my car now, and anxious to get this transaction behind me. Before I could even get ready to go to the garage, one of the men who worked there called about a car that had just been brought in the previous day as a trade-in. He knew I was going to trade soon, and he wanted us to see this car right away. Tony couldn't get up to the garage that morning, so the man drove it down for us to check it out. There was no doubt that this was a MUCH better car than the others I'd looked at, and it was in beautiful condition. It was just slightly over what I'd intended to pay, but this car was definitely worth the small addition to the cost.

I was thrilled! Immediately I assumed that THIS was why I hadn't been able to trade my car in before. They didn't HAVE this car until now. This car was perfect for me, so the car was returned to the dealership with the announcement that it was sold. As I drove my old car across town that morning, a very small town I might add, my car sputtered and died three times along the way. I'd hold up traffic each time, until I could get it started again. Talk about embarrassing! I was in a panic, wondering if my car would even make it TO the garage, or if I'd end up walking.

As I was approaching my destination, the word "Dilemma" appeared in the air in front of my face. I verbally dismissed the " dilemma" from my situation, and kept on going. I had really pushed this car to it's limit. I breathed a sigh of relief, and whispered a grateful "Thank You, Lord", as I pulled into the lot across the street from the dealership's office. I'd made it, but not a moment too soon. My car shut ITSELF off when I pulled into the lot, with such a sound of finality that I knew it had just expelled it's last dying breath. But I had gotten it there, and although they knew at the garage about the trouble I'd been having with it, I was almost sure they didn't know that it was now, in my estimation, ready for burial.

I went into the office to get started on the paperwork. Everything was going smoothly until I was asked for my license and registration. I opened my purse to retrieve my wallet, only to find that my wallet was curiously slimmer in my hand than usual. It was usually bursting at the seams because of all the cards and papers I kept stuffed into it, but it felt strangely light today. I opened it to find that half my cards and papers were missing, so I began taking things out of my purse, thinking they must have fallen out, and worked their way to the bottom. While the car dealer sat there patiently, I removed article after article from my purse, and placed the items on the chair beside me. By the time I got to the bottom, I felt my chest tightening. There were no cards in the bottom of my purse, either.

I told the dealer that my purse must have upset in the cupboard where I kept it at home, and apparently I hadn't noticed. I assured the dealer that my husband would find my cards, and bring them to me. I was given a phone to use to call home, but my phone rang and rang, and no one answered. I tried again, and still no answer. It looked like I'd have to go home and get my cards myself.

My next dilemma, I realized, would be having to go through the embarrassment of trying to resurrect a dead car in front of everyone at the garage. I was dreading this embarrassment, but

I knew I had to face this, and get it over with. Wanting to cry, I started walking toward the door, and to my deceased vehicle, when I was interrupted by the voice of the car dealer. "Vicki, I saw one of the guys out there a few minutes ago transferring the license plate. Your car has no plate on it now, so would you mind taking the new car instead?" he asked matter-of-factly. WOULD I MIND? I felt like a man on death row who had just heard from the governor. I happily got into the new car instead, promising to be back with my information, and thanking God all the way home for saving me any further embarrassment. I had been at the garage over the lunch hour, and now I was happily headed home in my soon-to-be new car to retrieve my cards and return to the garage to finish my paperwork, and make this trade official When I got to my house, I went straight to the cupboard in the kitchen that usually housed my purse, and opened the door. To my shock, which quickly turned to horror, there was nothing there. I looked everywhere, but still nothing. Where could my license and registration BE? This was not at all funny. I began looking in other parts of the house now, anywhere that I may have set my purse any time recently, and could find nothing. I panicked again, realizing that without the information I needed, I would have to take the car back, and wouldn't be able to even bring the old one home. I honestly believed that the old car wouldn't start again without some help from the car doctors at the garage. This was humiliating! I was home for about twenty minutes, looking through everything I could think of, when I finally surrendered to the inevitable. I was without wheels.

I didn't know how long it would take to get copies of my drivers license and registration, but I knew I'd never be able to complete the deal until then. Crushed, I picked up my purse, and walked out onto my front porch. I would now have to go back to the dealership and cancel the transaction, after all.

Solemnly stepping out onto the porch, I was surprised to see the mail truck coming down the street. I glanced at my watch. It was only one-thirty in the afternoon. We never got our mail before four o'clock, so what was the mailman doing here so early? He never did that. I watched as he pulled up in front of my house.

As I continued to watch, he got out of the truck with a large manila envelope in his hand. Everything inside me leaped for joy as he walked toward my mailbox, while in the spirit I heard "There it is!". I knew my papers were in there, but I didn't know how I knew…I just knew. I ran to meet the mailman, and told him I'd take that envelope, and he handed it over with a smile. I ran back into the house, anxiously opened the envelope, and dumped the contents on the table. Yes, it was all there. My cards, my pictures, my LICENSE, my REGISTRATION! Everything that had been missing out of my wallet had just arrived in the mail. But…WHY? I picked up the envelope now, and turned it over. The return address on the envelope was from some address in… OHIO?

It took me a moment to make the connection. This was the truck stop we had eaten lunch at TWO WEEKS AGO, when we were coming home from church out there. This was incredible.

Now I found the letter that was still inside the envelope. It was a very nice letter from a lady in management at that truck stop. She said someone had found these things in the parking lot a couple of weeks ago, and had brought them in. When they saw what these things were, they had put them into the envelope to return to me, but the envelope had been laid on top of a file cabinet, and overlooked until now. She was apologizing for the delay in returning them. I wasn't at all concerned about the delay. The only thing I cared about was that they were here NOW. I was so thankful that they would take the time to return them at all. I got in the new car and headed straight to the garage, where the paperwork was finished, and I became that car's official owner.

When I was finished at the dealership that day, and was driving home, I started realizing what a miracle it was that I had gotten those pictures and cards back. The even greater miracle was that they were intact, for now I was remembering that day at the truck stop.

We had pulled into the parking lot by the restaurant during the first stages of a torrential downpour. We had all jumped out of the car as fast as we could to get into the restaurant, and away from that pelting rain. I had caught the handle of my purse on the door handle when I was getting out, and my purse had upset. I'd retrieved it quickly, along with a couple of things that had fallen out, but we were in such a hurry because of the rainstorm, that it never occurred to me to check any further. I just grabbed the stuff and ran! How these things, that had apparently slid under the car unnoticed, ever survived the amount of water that ran through that parking lot that day was a mystery to me, but there'd been no damage done to any of these things.

Now I was beginning to understand why I hadn't been able to go to the dealership any sooner than what I had. Not only had a better car come along, but God knew all along where my license and registration were, and I hadn't even been aware that they were missing. He also knew when they'd arrive. He had kept everything in perfect timing, as usual, by keeping ME in check.

I've never been more aware of His ability to coordinate time as I have been since that event. I was completely in awe of how He had handled everything, and how much He had been in control over the whole situation, since I'd upset my purse in a parking lot in another state. Any time I find myself becoming anxious concerning when anything will happen, I just remind myself of who's in charge, and I also remind myself that He's got the script. He won't let us miss anything, but better yet, it won't come too soon, or too late. His timing is brilliant, and before we can even have a "mishap", He's already got it covered, and all's right with our world. It's easier, knowing this, to become the trusting children He wants us to be. And we can, because we have a very capable Father to rely on.

chapter 30

GOD DOESN'T
HEAL HALFWAY

It was not my habit to visit doctors, simply because that habit had not been established while I was growing up. If you were at death's door, a doctor would be consulted, otherwise you braved the problem on your own, using whatever home remedies had been passed down through the generations. When I got older, a doctor was considered only if you were either pregnant, or appeared to be dying, and I didn't find myself in either of these qualifying situations often. An occasional headache was certainly not ranked among life-threatening reasons to consult a professional. I had the occasional headache, like anyone else, but they never really caused a problem, other than to be a temporary nuisance, and they were nothing that a couple of aspirin couldn't conquer. There came a time, however, during my second marriage, when I began experiencing a different kind of headaches. I was beginning to develop migraines.

They had begun as only an occasional shock to my system, occurring no more frequently than once every two or three months. During the next couple of years, they had progressed in intensity and frequency, until I was now totally incapacitated for three, sometimes four, days at a time, every other week. Now THIS was becoming a problem. If you've ever experienced a migraine, you know how devastating they can be. From the time they start, until they finally let go, you have zero tolerance for any light, sound, or movement, for any of these things will cause excruciating pain, far beyond what aspirin, or anything ELSE for that matter, can relieve. They are actually paralyzing in their severity.

These headaches were more than just a temporary nuisance, but I would get through them, and be so grateful when they subsided, so I could get on with my life.

It was interesting how they would start, for this onslaught of pain would begin with what felt like someone whacking the base of my skull with the blunt end of an axe. Within seconds from the initial blow, the relentless pain would begin. I don't know why it never occurred to me to bring the subject of these headaches to our prayer group, but I never had. I suppose I just didn't feel that they warranted any more attention than what they got when I was experiencing them. It was bad enough that they were interfering with my life a couple of times a month, and I wasn't going to allow them to interfere with anything else when they WEREN'T beating up my brain.

During this time, some members of our group had opened up a new local chapter of a Full-Gospel women's organization, and we were holding monthly meetings. The headaches had never interfered with the meetings, but they were definitely interfering with the rest of my life. One of the major triggers that would bring on the "axe", as I called it, was to sit down with my Bible and begin to read. The last migraine headache I would ever experience had started just that way again.

I hadn't completed a full minute of reading before the axe struck. I had just enough time to grab some extra-strength aspirin, get the lights off, any noise turned off, and lay down with a pillow over my face to keep any other light out, before the pain took over, paralyzing me for the next couple of days. I was more than a little disgusted by now with this problem, and I told the Lord that evening, while I lay in my darkened bedroom, not daring to move, that something had to be done about this. In a whisper, I stated my case to Him. I was useless to God, and others, in this condition, and I told Him so. Now that I had come to a point of not even being able to read without bringing on a two or three day siege, I had decided it was time for a decision to be made. "Cure me or kill me", I earnestly requested, and told Him I didn't care which way it went, for living like this wasn't living at all. He said nothing.

A couple of days after this last painful bout, everyone who was involved in the working part of those monthly meetings gathered in my home for a prayer meeting to prepare for the monthly meeting that was scheduled to take place the following week. We intended to bring the subject of next week's meeting before God to see what needed to be taken care of in prayer before the actual event. The evening took a different direction than what we had planned, and we ended up praying for each person there, one at a time, and I was the last in line.

No sooner had someone put their hand on my forehead, and the girls began to pray in the spirit, than someone else said, "Is anyone here having a problem with headaches? When you all started to pray, I got an instant headache."

"Well, yes, I've been having some headaches lately." I said. No one but Joyce really knew about the migraines, because I hadn't bothered to mention them before. As soon as I acknowledged that I had a problem with headaches, the other girl's headache disappeared.

They resumed the prayer for me, and someone in the group said that they saw in the spirit that there was a terrible pressure around me, and as soon as she started to speak, I saw a huge red vice, like my father had had in his garage, as though it were turned on it's side, and my body was laying on the bottom part of the vice grip. The top grip of the vice was being lowered down to meet the one on the bottom, and the problem was that my limp body was right between the two. I could easily see that if this went on much longer I would be crushed.

We remained in prayer, with them asking for healing, but nothing seemed to happen, so with that, the meeting was over for the evening, and I went to bed that night apologizing to God for the fact that we had prayed for one another that evening, and had forgotten to pray about the meeting that would be held next week, and after all, that's what we had gotten together for in the first place. He informed me that, by praying for the people, we had already taken care of the meeting, for the only thing that is important about any meeting IS the people. I laughed about this little straightening out, and went to bed.

The following week would find us early at the meeting place, setting up tables and chairs, and preparing for the speaker to arrive. We were really excited about the speaker who was coming from Ohio that morning to lead this meeting. She taught a lot about healing, having experienced a dramatic healing of her own. She had been a nightclub singer before she met the Lord, and we had heard this lady sing before. We were all in awe of her voice, but even more in awe of her powerful love for Jesus, and her confidence in His power to heal.

It was time for the meeting to begin, and the speaker hadn't arrived yet, so it was decided that we would go ahead and begin the meeting and pray that she was alright, and that she'd get there safely. We had opened with prayer, and some announcements, and went ahead into a time of singing. While we were singing, I became aware of a powerful presence that entered the room at the same time I heard a car pulling into the graveled parking lot outside. This powerful anointing filled the room now, and I knew the speaker had arrived. She came in apologizing for being late, but she wasn't really late. She was right on time to begin what she had come for.

She told her story, and taught in a most amazing way about the power of God to heal anything, and when she was finished, she said she would be available now to pray with anyone who had come for prayer. We finished the meeting with another song and, as the speaker now prepared to minister to others, I began to close up the registration table. Suddenly the speaker was asking for everyone to please listen. We all stopped anything we were doing in order to give her our full attention.

She said the Lord had just spoken something to her that she needed to share before she even started to pray with anyone. He had told her that someone here was having a problem with severe headaches. I immediately scanned the room, looking for the person who would come forward with this problem, sympathizing with whomever it was, because I, myself, knew all too well what kind of pain they were enduring. No one moved.

Then she said "The Lord is telling me right now, whoever you are, that Satan has devised a plan to destroy you, and today the

Lord is removing these headaches, and He's also removing the pressure that has been causing them." When she said that, the vision of the vice appeared in a momentary flash, and then was gone again. When I saw it, I now realized that it was ME He was talking about. I'd no sooner connected with that realization, and whispered "Why... that's me!", when a wave of what felt like a gentle electric current pulsed all the way through me, and I knew I had just been healed. I never said a word, but sat right back down on my chair, thanking God for what He had just done.

The speaker now began praying with people while the rest of us put the room back the way we had found it, but when I finished what I had to do, I waited until the speaker was finished with others, then went to tell her that what she had heard from God had been for me. I had approached her with the intention of thanking her for being available for us that day, and to my surprise, she was standing there thanking me. She was thanking me for telling her what God had done because of her speaking what He had told her, because she said it's difficult to give a word like that to a crowd and have no one acknowledge anything about it. Speakers and teachers, she said, need confirmation, too.

I went happily on my way that day, knowing that the siege of headaches was over. It was about six pain-free weeks later, while I was standing at my kitchen sink washing dishes, that the old familiar "axe" hit the base of my skull again. My past experience with that initial blow was always to drop everything and prepare for pain. When the "axe" struck this time, one instant question went through my mind. Did I dare try to finish washing what was already in my hand, or should I drop everything NOW, and head for the sofa, before the pain started.

That reactive thought no sooner zipped through my mind, when something stood right up inside me, and literally turned my head to the counter top to my right, where I became aware of a presence perched right on that counter in the corner of my kitchen, not three feet away from where I was standing. I couldn't see it with my physical eyes, but everything in me was totally aware that something was sitting on the counter. I could feel the energy of it. I now addressed the presence in a tone of voice that said there'll be no game-playing going on here! The statement of authority that came unhesitatingly out of my mouth right then made me know that it was the Holy Spirit within me who had immediately risen to this occasion. And it was HIM who was addressing the situation now. "Oh, no you don't! This isn't REAL. God already healed me, and He doesn't HEAL half-way!" In that very instant, the presence in the corner, and the pressure that had already begun to encompass my head, vanished simultaneously, and have never to this day, years later, returned.

I don't know which had impressed me the most...the healing itself, or the victory against the lie that tried to invade a few weeks later. All I know is that it was all done by God, and I am one grateful patient.

chapter 31
THE STARVING ARTIST

An artist paints what he sees, the very thing that has impressed itself upon him. He takes great pains to make sure that every detail is exact, so he can share with the world his finished product. If he has been impacted by a scene, he holds it in his heart until the opportunity comes when he can transfer it onto a canvas. We are all artists, whether we realize it or not, and some of us have never picked up a brush!

I became an artist without a brush years ago. If you think you're not an artist, think again. God is a creator, and He made man in His image. In other words, He gave man qualities that He has. He creates, and so He has given us the same ability, and whether we're aware of it or not, we are creating all the time. He thought, then He spoke, and it WAS. We are no different. We think, then we speak, and it IS. Sometimes people say that they're not "creative", but I beg to differ.

I carried my paintbrush, as did my friends, every where I went. It was my mouth. My colors were my words. And everywhere I went, I found canvasses to paint on, and that was the minds of anyone who would listen. I lived in a society of potential Picasso's like myself, where each painted freely their distorted view of life, competing for recognition in the form of sympathy, comfort and pity. The most highly regarded award of all was what we sought, that being the Blue Ribbon Prize for having the most traumatic problem on the block. What better way to take center stage and have all eyes upon you while you paint for everyone your finest work, consisting of the most morbid details of your misunderstood, misused and abused life in the midst of your most recent dilemma.

Some paint with tears, some with rage, but myself, I had studied my art, and had found that adding a touch of humor to my paintings was a much more effective way to hold the attention of my audience. People love to laugh, so I had developed a tremendously funny way of describing my life, while I painted horrifying scenes in the minds of others, allowing the humor to insure that the paint would set.

By using these tactics, I got the recognition I was looking for, in the form of a comforting hand upon my shoulder, or a reassuring hug from the other artists, but little did I know that these paintings would only serve to fill the dungeon-like halls of minds already filled to near-capacity with paintings of their own disasters. By humorously painting a fresh portrait of my poor pitiful self, I automatically inspired the other artists in the group, so they would now begin to drag out their old paintings from their hall of memories, and the parade of artwork would begin.

One by one, we would scrutinize each detail of each painting. The awe-filled words "How did you ever survive that?" is like applause to the artist's ears, and we now bow the martyr's bow before our audience. Whoever would have received THAT word of acclaim had won the prize for the day. The honor from hell.

Our human tendency is to be the best at what we do, even if what we do is destructive to ourselves and others.

I prided myself on being an excellent painter, although I wasn't at all consciously aware of what I was doing at the time. I know now that the others didn't realize that that was what THEY were doing either, when it was THEIR turn to wield the brush.

Why did I say that we took pride in being the winner of these macabre sessions? Because there is a morbid sense of satisfaction that you get from sitting back and watching your audience once you've finished. They become spellbound as they sit, wide-eyed, looking at your artwork. They are not only stunned, but shocked, intrigued, and hypnotized by the effect your painting has had on them. How you must be suffering, they're now thinking, and you are, of course, but at least there's that sense of satisfaction knowing that others now KNOW how much you're suffering, Oh, the praise you have coming to you now, for you are truly a survivor. You are an honest-to-goodness citizen of martyrdom. God forbid that one of the other artists would display a more impacting painting than the one you have just done, however, distracting your audience from their new-found leader, which, of course, is you. You, as an accomplished artist, are perfectly prepared for this type of pitfall. You dive into your personal gallery to retrieve one of your most effective memories, and put that on display. You have become a talented entertainer, because you have discovered a power within you, in the midst of your misery, to captivate your friends and neighbors and draw their attention solely to your pain. The fact that you can laugh while you're entertaining in this way earns you even more honor, because of your bravery, and you accept the admiration of your friends with feigned humility. You've become so creative in your art that, should you notice the attention of the others waning, you simply draw them back by pointing out a detail or two that they may have overlooked the first time. You rest assured that you have earned the title "Artiste Magnifique!"

Although you are aware of the fact that you would like to have a happier life, you know that you have no solutions for your problems, so under the guise of looking for answers, you entertain with paintings. If any of your audience may have had a solution to offer, they can't think of it now, for they've been totally swept away by every stroke of your brush.

You've become a sensationalist concerning your own life, and although you live in despair in the absence of solutions, you settle for this phony field of entertainment. After all, you really must do the best with what you have, and you have pain. So you opt for center stage in a very cruel play, but what the heck, at least you're the star.

What a performance you've learned to give. You know just when to express anger, and just when to cry (for the sake of your audience, of course), and it's amazing how your little circle of friends have learned to take their cues from you. They laugh when you want them to, they cry when it's appropriate, and they angrily defend you to others when you, the poor victim, are unable to defend yourself. My, how loved you feel. This alone should make your life complete, but still there's that undercurrent of quiet hopelessness that you've had to learn to live with. This subtle undercurrent leaves you with an empty feeling when the gallery is closed, and the audience has all gone home. Oh, you know they'll still be discussing you and your latest dilemma with great compassion and concern, but they're not with you now, so it's just not the same.

You're noticing that it's been harder lately to draw them into the gallery. It seems you've displayed these paintings so many times, that there aren't really any more details left to reveal, short of lying, and wouldn't that make you as bad as some of the people in your paintings? Now that your friends are gone for the day, there's not much left for you to do but sit and stare glumly at the painting you've just created, now hanging in your mind alongside the others that you have brought out of your secret gallery and re-hung in your consciousness.

An awful picture comes to mind now of what appears to have once been a beautiful garden, now overgrown with weeds. It looks terribly neglected, with only a couple of brownish, dried up flowers that you think you see amidst the rubble. You see it in your mind's eye, and wonder why it's there. The only thing that seems to be thriving is a great, huge thistle, so big that it looks more like a tree. There are smaller thistles dotting the scene, and they all seem to be doing well, but they appear to have choked out what might have been beautiful at one time. You'd paint this scene, but it's much too disgusting to want to reproduce, so you shake your head and toss it out of your sight for now. It's been a long day for this particular artist. It's time to pack up the gallery and go to bed.

This was me before I met the Lord. This was also me in the beginning of my walk with Him. I was a starving artist. I wanted the abundant life that the Bible promises, but I couldn't break through all those paintings in my mind to get a clear picture of what it was that God was really offering, no matter how dearly I loved Him. Many around me were the same. The reason that this happens is because we've been so impacted with such vivid negative experiences, that they have been stamped on our psyche like so many paintings done in non-erasable colors. These traumas control us. They are lodged in our minds. We need to get them out of there, but we don't know that, and if we did, we don't know how. God says He loves us and we try to believe that, but in the subconscious mind hangs the deeply imbedded impression of an unlovable human being. So we try and try to believe that God loves us, memorizing scripture after scripture, until we have our conscious mind convinced, only to have the monster impression in our subconscious mind gobble up the thought of our being loved, and we're right back at square one again.

The Bible says that a double-minded man receives nothing, and I used to think that meant my problem was that I kept changing my mind. God loves me, or maybe He doesn't, this is good, or maybe it's bad, I can do this, or maybe not. I had decided that indecision was my problem, until God took me deeper, and showed me where that problem was really coming from. Indecision was only a branch of that tree. The root was the negative image I had of myself, deeply imbedded in my subconscious mind, always overpowering the good things I was putting into my consciousness.

So there you have it! There wasn't anything wrong with my decisions, for my decision was to live a life pleasing to God. I just didn't realize I had two minds, and that the one I wasn't even aware of, the subconscious, was at war with my decisions, and overpowering them every time. In order to receive the things of God, we need to have these minds of ours in agreement. The trick is to get the negatives out of the subconscious that argue against who God says we are. But do we do that? Like I said, we don't know how. Worse yet, we're making things worse by the way we think, under the invisible influence of the subconscious mind, and by the way we talk, and we didn't even know it.

There is a power that we have over this situation, and that is the power of prayer. Since those negative memories are part of our very makeup, we can ask the Lord to remove the controlling POWER of those memories. He can certainly do that, and that's a step in the right direction. In the next chapter I'm going to open this up a little more to show how we make those memories even stronger, and how they gain MORE power over us, when we wanted the opposite, and then I'll show you how God showed me how to change this. There really IS hope. Happy reading!

chapter 32
WATERING THISTLES

I once watched a TV commentary on an Aboriginal tribe. The men had permitted a reporter to accompany them on a hunting trip, in order to find out, firsthand, why they were such successful hunters. Along toward evening, they had speared a female giraffe, and were now tracking her. Since it would soon be getting dark, making it impossible for them to continue, they made a camp for the night, to rest and be refreshed to continue the tracking in the morning. They talked much while they unwound from the excitement of the day, and surprisingly enough, they never once mentioned the giraffe. The reporter, there only to observe, didn't question this until the hunting trip was over.

They had gotten the giraffe the following morning, and it was after that that the reporter commented on their silence the night before concerning the animal. What he was told, was that they never SPOKE of her, for they didn't want to EMPOWER her. Now, what has that got to do with watering thistles, you ask? Hold on… let me explain.

I had been looking for answers as usual. I had a situation in my life that, no matter how much I prayed about it, only seemed to be getting worse. During my search for a solution, I came across, in Proverbs 14:1 in my Living Bible, where it says, "A wise woman builds her house, while a foolish woman tears hers down by her own efforts." I asked the Lord what women USE to build their house, or tear it down, and He said "Words". I had recently listened to someone teaching on the power of the spoken word, and how words go out of our mouths like radio waves, and land on their target every time. I thought I now understood all that God meant by "words" being used to build or tear down, but since I had asked, He decided to enlighten me even further by adding "Stop watering thistles".

I watched as an animated vision appeared. I saw a lady standing in the middle of a lush garden, full of wonderful, colorful flowers. There were so many flowers that the only way to move around in this garden was by way of a system of narrow paths that allowed just enough room for a single person to walk through. I watched her begin to walk along one of those paths, stopping here and there to enjoy the fragrance emanating from the different groups of plants. At one point, she stopped abruptly. Frowning, she bent down to look at her ankle, where I noticed a tiny drop of blood oozing from a scratch that she had just received. She had apparently brushed her ankle against something hidden amongst the flowers.

She then began looking through the flowers to see what had scratched her, and as she separated flowers and searched, she found what she'd been looking for. She spread the plants apart in one spot to reveal a small thistle growing right along the edge. It was such a harmless-looking little plant, but apparently it had just enough little prickly outgrowths to have caught her ankle, and her attention. If she hadn't felt the sting of it, I don't think it would have been noticed at all, because of its dwarfed size compared to the flowers.

As she bent over the thistle, the trunk of her body took on the form of a large watering can, and her head took on the appearance of a spout. What a humorous sight she was now. While she remained in this position, a spray of tiny light particles began to flow in a slow, steady spray from her spout-like face onto the thistle. It sprayed gently and continuously, as though it were water. She continued to hold the flowers back away from it for a while, while she turned her head this way and that, examining the thistle thoroughly. All the while, this soft spray of light continued to flow, and the thistle continued to absorb the spray. She let go of the flowers and stood up. When she stood, and the flowers went back to their normal position, she once again took on a normal appearance. I could now see the thistle among the flowers, but I hadn't been able to see it before. It seemed as though it had grown.

She turned and ran down the path to the edge of her garden, and motioned to a neighbor to come. When the two returned to the thistle, they both examined it. As they stooped to examine the invader, they BOTH took on the appearance of watering cans. A soft spray of light was coming from both of them now, onto the thistle. As they began to TALK about it, an even larger spray of light emanated from them. The thistle was flourishing under all this attention, I noticed, for it was absorbing every ray. As I watched, it increased in size. While they studied the plant, other neighbors came by, and two more ladies joined them to discuss the problem. As their attention was brought to the thistle, sprays of light from these additional ladies joined the sprays already coming from the others, and it was all directed to the thistle. As they talked, the thistle became even larger. The others finally left, and the lady stood alone now, looking at this larger than life plant. It had grown from a tiny plant to a thistle the size of a small tree. This little tiny problem had now become a very LARGE problem! And even worse, the flowers that had been so lush and brilliantly colored, had seemed to pale a little while they talked about the thistle. The flowers now appeared to be weaker and more frail than before.

The vision remained as the Lord began to speak to me concerning what I had just watched. He said that the lady's garden was her life, and that it had been filled with all sorts of wonderful things that He had provided for her. The thistle was a tiny problem that had cropped up, in the midst of all that beauty. She had felt a momentary discomfort, that sent her looking for the problem When she found it, she had focused all of her attention on it, even drawing other's attention to it, never once commenting on the flowers.

He said that we are filled with life-giving energy, and when the lady focused her attention on the tiny problem, she was feeding it life energy, and causing it to become stronger. As she talked about it with others, they joined her in focusing on the problem, and each time they thought about it and talked about it, they were feeding it even MORE vital energy. He said this is the mistake we make with problems. What needed to be done, He said, was simply to pull it out by the root at the moment it was discovered, and it would never have been able to grow. The problem was that focusing on the problem also caused her to neglect to feed that life energy to the beauty in her life that the flowers represented.

I knew, as He explained this to me, that I was the lady in the garden. I was guilty of dwelling on problems, and it was true. They did seem to get bigger. I remembered times when I would notice something annoying, and think about it and talk about it until it had finally become an overwhelming problem in my life. No wonder Philippians 4:8 in the Living Bible instructs, " Fix your thoughts on what is true and good and right. Think about things that are pure and lovely, and dwell on the fine, good things in others." Whatever you dwell on will surely grow, and not only in your life, but in the lives of those whose gardens you're helping to water.

If you want a garden full of thistles, just do what I was doing. Keep dwelling on the problems. And better yet, just keep talking about them! Guaranteed, your garden will grow, but I doubt you're going to like it. Myself, I decided I'd better start focusing my watering-can mouth more on the good things in my life. That hasn't been easy sometimes, when I've just received an "ouch" from a brand new thistle, but if I can remember that whatever I water will grow, I've found it much easier to stop myself before I've created another tree. Trees are MUCH harder to remove. And worse yet, when fully matured, they will start popping up baby thistles all around them, a whole NEW crop of problems. The problems in my life have lessened, and the good things in my life have increased, since I learned this principal.

Before I met the Lord, my friends and I would get together on a regular basis, just to water one another's thistles, then we'd wonder why our lives were just so difficult. AFTER I met the Lord, my Christian friends and I would get together, and discuss our problems, and pray about them, and discuss them some more, and pray about them again, and wonder why our lives were just so DIFFICULT. Gee! Notice any similarity here? Once God showed me the truth about the garden, it was easier and easier to stop that kind of conversation that was only making our lives worse. "No more watering thistles!" became the theme of our get-togethers now, and we began to water the flowers in one another's lives. We called our get-togethers now, "Praise time." We'd all leave that time together happier. Is it any wonder why?

I've had times when a thistle, upon discovery, would seem so overwhelming that I couldn't see past it to find a flower to water. When this has happened, I've had to, in faith, re-focus my watering process anyway, by simply thanking God for the flowers I know are there. I would thank Him for electricity, a roof over my head, food on the table, health, my kids, indoor plumbing, my car, my job, my friends, etc., ANYTHING I could think of, to get my focus off the problem. Do you know what happens when you do that? The thistle seems to shrink! It loses it's "overwhelming" power. We can't completely ignore our problems, because all problems, big and small, are real, and need to be dealt with. (If you're noticing a thistle, you can be assured that it has taken root.) To ignore them completely would be to live our lives in denial, giving the problem permission to grow at a steady pace, undisturbed.

The best solution I have found to getting rid of thistles, is to find one true friend I can pray with, and together we ask God to expose the root, which I then renounce, thus removing the cause of the problem. The Bible says that if any two agree on something, it will be done by our Father in Heaven. If we agree then, that God will uproot it, we can rest assured that He will, as we move on to the business of watering our flowers. Even better yet, throw out the thistle, and plant a flower there. What is the flower? The solution, of course! Wouldn't it be more fun to water that?

Look around you. How IS your garden doing? If you've found that thistles seem to be overtaking your life, then it's time to change the direction of your energy flow. I thank God for the vision of the garden. It wasn't enough for me to read that I was to think on good things. I knew that, but I just wasn't getting the whole picture. I needed a visual aid to help me understand. My Father God, who knows me better than I know myself, KNEW that, so He, being the provider of all that we'll ever need, gave me that visual aid, so I could understand completely. Otherwise, I could have still been living in a wasteland. When we learn the lesson of the thistles, and learn to tend our gardens the way God intended, we'll find ourselves living in a garden of Eden situation in NO time.

Find a thistle, pluck it out, and plant a flower there. We pluck the thistles out by going to God to find the root. An uprooted thistle will just dry up, and won't get the chance to scratch ANYONE, let alone multiply in your garden. In the meantime, as you focus on the flowers, they continue to grow to such an enlarged state, with roots so strong that a little thistle couldn't get a foothold if it had to.

chapter 33
THE GYMNASIUM

Once our prayer group had gotten God's point concerning the order of prayer, the only word to describe what happened from that point on was "GROWTH"! I don't mean that the numbers in attendance grew, although they did, but what I mean is that we began to grow UP as we experienced the higher understanding in God's mind. I've often said that the greatest thing I'd ever come to know concerning praying for anyone was that, on my own, I didn't know anything. To THINK we know, is much different from really knowing. We had learned how to go to God to get the truth.

There is nothing more disheartening for a wounded member of the Body of Christ, than a generic prayer. Specific "needs" need specific instructions. If we don't find the root of the problem, we can pray that they be healed, just to find them back again, and wounded again, in just the same way.

Assumption prayer is nothing more than a double-barreled waste of time. Not only will assumption pray inaccurately, but we can pray in agreement a very nice request, and it can be done, not only complicating matters for our poor prayer victim, but it keeps the REAL issue from being dealt with, even longer. A brother, in a pit of despair, doesn't need a nice warm blanket and a pillow prayed to him in that pit. He needs to be brought OUT of the pit, and the opening to the pit CLOSED, so he never falls into it again!

Let's say we have to get from one town to another, and it's important that we get there as soon as possible. We are in our vehicle, going after an antidote for a deadly disease that has stricken someone in the family, so there's no time to waste. There are two different roads that we can take to get to our destination, thirty miles away. One is shorter than the other, and we know that others have traveled this road successfully before, so we assume it's the best road to take, since time is of the essence. This road is about five miles shorter than the other, thus saving us precious time.

Assuming that we've made the right choice, we fire up the vehicle, and go racing down the road. Everything is going well, until we're about a mile from our destination, when we find that the bridge we need to cross has been closed. Worse yet, it's been barricaded. We'll never be able to get through the barricade, and even if we could, we see that the reason for the barricade is that part of the bridge has been washed away. Now we'll have to turn around and go back, doubling our driving time to nowhere. Then we'll have to start over, taking the longer road this time. How much time was just wasted? That's what happens when we assume anything in prayer. We pray and pray and pray, only to end up nowhere, and having to go back and start again.

Going to God for direction in prayer is the same as asking the highway authority which road to take. It's only those in authority who know the true conditions in any situation. Had we called on the highway authority as to which road to take in the first place, he would have told us to take the longer road, knowing that the bridge was out. Had we gone to God in prayer concerning a brother's needs, He would have told us which direction to take in prayer, saving us and our brother much wasted time and pain. Entering into spirit prayer will connect us with the one in authority. It's then much easier to see which way to go to get the antidote.

We began praying for one another in this fashion. We spent time praying for each one in attendance, waiting to see what God had in mind for each individual. It was the greatest learning time we'd ever spent, while God Himself opened up new possibilities, and new worlds to us. We received gifts of great knowledge from the One who has it all, and we continued to grow in understanding. There were many times of deliverance for all. When we think of deliverance, we sometimes think of great demonic monsters that we have to be set free from, but we found that each deliverance was from anything that stood in the way of our being free to be all that we were meant to be.

There came a day when we were questioned as to why we prayed for one another week after week. Shouldn't we, after all, be praying for the condition of our world, and all the problems in it? The comment that was made suggested that we were just being selfish for wanting to pray for one another all the time. Since we didn't really have an answer to the question, Joyce and I went to God concerning the matter. When He answered, He began His answer with just one word. "Gymnasium."

That made no sense to us, but having learned that He doesn't waste time with idle words, we spent more time with Him, pursuing an explanation. What He told us was that He had established for us a spiritual gymnasium. It was a place for all of us who were young and inexperienced, or older and inexperienced, to come together to build our spiritual muscles. He said it was a place of preparation. He was preparing us for war, and warriors must be trained, and warriors must become strong. Satisfied that we were doing what He wanted, we didn't question any further, for now we understood. We had prayed as we were led by the Spirit, but now we knew WHY we were praying this way. We were being groomed for spiritual warfare, and we were training with one another. It was His purpose and plan, and He was training us. We weren't playing church here…we were becoming stronger members of the church here.

chapter 34
... AND DELIVER US FROM EVIL

The Lord spoke to me one day saying, "Hell hath torment." I thought about this statement for a moment before He spoke again. "Fear hath torment," was His second statement.. I already knew that yes, the Bible said that in 1 John 4:18 (KJV). But why had He just spoken these two different statements? Then He said something that startled me. All He said was "They are one in the same."

Oh, My! He had just snapped a light switch on in my mind. Why hadn't I seen this before? I sat there amazed. It would never have occurred to me to put these two statements together, and He had just turned my entire thought process around with three simple statements.

As I continued to pray quietly in the spirit, it all started to fall into place. Of course. Jesus died to deliver us from Hell. He died to deliver us from FEAR. We were experiencing Hell every time we were afraid. It was then that I realized that the most needed deliverance that we all had to experience was deliverance from all the fears that were already in us.

As this quiet understanding began to permeate my mind, scriptures began to come together for me like so many scattered puzzle pieces. They were forming a picture of what it was that the Lord was really intending to do. Another scripture that came to mind was, "If we confess our sins, He is faithful and just to forgive us our sins and cleanse us from all unrighteousness."(1 John 1:9, Living Bible) Where we carry fear, rather than faith, we are "missing the mark", or "sinning", for what we fear, we cannot love. As the picture became clearer yet, another scripture gave added depth to my perception. "For God hath not given us a spirit of

FEAR, but of power, and of love, and of a sound mind." (2 Tim. 1:7 , Living Bible). Yep, It made sense now! Any time we reacted in a way that was not displaying power, love, and a sound mind, we were displaying FEAR. Now I could understand that the thing that kept us from being able to love as God loves, unconditionally, was nothing more than any fear that had ever been instilled in us. Those fears, that Hell, were already part of us, and in order to set us free to be the children we were meant to be, we would simply have to start identifying our fears, confessing them to Him, and He would be faithful and just to set us free from all that was not right, in other words, all in us that agreed with Hell, or fear, rather than love, which is God Himself.

It became clear to me that the very uncomfortable things that I had to experience were not things to be prayed away, but rather to be worked with. These were circumstances that my Father was sending my way in order to bring these fears up from within me, so I could identify them, confess them to Him, let Him remove them, and finally be free.

After this understanding came, I found myself approaching problems in a whole new light. I came to understand that all of my angers and frustrations about ANY circumstance in my life were simply based on a fear that had been touched in me. If we're not afraid of anything, we live in peace. If we're full of hidden fears, we live in torment, still residents of Hell.

Fears disguise themselves as anger, rage, sadness, frustration, depression, nervousness, anxiety attacks, indignation, etc., but the root of all these negative emotions is still FEAR. Fears thrive in darkness, and just let God send a circumstance our way that isn't comfortable, and you can bet the discomfort that we begin to feel is the first rumbling of a fear getting ready to erupt. Let it! You don't have to voice it to others, you just have to admit it's there, find out what kind of fear it is, confess it to God, and be done with it. The bonus is, that when you go to God with these things, He will remove the fear, and replace it with His truth, ensuring that that particular fear will never have a place to hide in you again, for His truth is LIGHT, and fears only dwell in darkness.

There are so many fears that we carry that we don't even know exist in us. I found that I was riddled with these blocks to love. We're afraid that people won't like us, then we're afraid they will, and if they like us, we're afraid they'll get to know us and change their minds. We're afraid to be too excited about the Lord in front of others for fear of ridicule. We're afraid of poverty, we're afraid of failure, we're afraid of success, and we're afraid of disease and death. We're afraid we love the wrong people, we're afraid we're going to look like fools, and we're afraid of loneliness. The most debilitating fear of all is the fear of following the leading of the Spirit within, for fear that we'll offend someone. You name it, and guaranteed, we'll fear it.

That stops when we learn the process of God for our deliverance, and when we stop trying to live a superficial religious life, and begin getting down to the business of getting cleaned up. God's got things for us to do in this world. We can't follow His Spirit, if we carry the restrictions of FEAR.

I developed the habit, when I got upset about anything, of getting quiet with God to identify the fear that was hidden in the upset, then just letting Him get rid of it. Life becomes much more productive when we live it in harmony with God.

As a close-knit prayer group, we let go of our fears, and we studied God, and we grew. We had entered basic training to become part of the army of God that we had been destined for. We had become an intercessory prayer group. There wasn't any problem that anyone could bring, that God wouldn't shed His light on. We became like a well-oiled praying machine. We were operating now with a "clearing house" attitude. When any of us were upset about anything, instead of going to God about the circumstance that had upset us, we now went to God to identify the FEAR that had caused our negative REACTION to that circumstance. We were doing some spiritual "spring cleaning", so to speak, clearing out, one by one, every fear... as our circumstances revealed them.

This clearing-out process was causing a lot of inner healing to take place. Old wounds were being exposed, brought to the light of God, where their power just disintegrated in His presence. The fact that we loved one another kept us patient with one another during this process, and little by little, we were gaining more strength in our own individual lives. Little by little, we were being healed, from the inside out.

chapter 35
THE MESS IN THE MIDDLE

As children of God, we're promised an abundant life, filled with peace, joy, and prosperity. I knew that by now. I read it all the time. I heard about it in church, and they taught about it on the TV ministries. The problem I was having, though, was that everything I was hearing that I possessed, and what I was actually displaying, were sometimes two different things entirely. If I were to be living this wonderful life now with the Lord in charge, and all these promises from God, then why was I having so many difficulties?

If we were to live in abundance, why was I dealing with such lack? If we were to live a prosperous life, then why was I always struggling with poverty? Peace and joy? I had them sometimes, but they just didn't ever seem to last long enough between times of turmoil. Don't get me wrong. My life wasn't a series of disasters any more, but it just wasn't the abundant life that I kept hearing about. Have you ever experienced that, or am I the only one?

If you've found this to be a problem in your life too, did you ever notice how easy it is to blame others for this? I did. Someone ELSE must be the problem. After all, we're doing the right things, just the way we're taught, aren't we? Then we SHOULD be enjoying all these wonderful gifts from God, so why AREN'T we? Since we're doing everything the way the Bible teaches, and our lives STILL aren't the way the Bible says they're supposed to be, we start looking around for an outside source to blame.

Have you ever heard anyone make any of the following statements? "If my spouse would just quit drinking, my life would finally be peaceful. If my children would just quit messing up their lives, I could QUIT worrying. If my spouse would just quit GAMBLING,

I'd be ABLE to live in prosperity. If my in-laws would just quit CRITCIZING me, I wouldn't HAVE this frustration. If my boss wasn't such a jerk, I'd HAVE a better attitude at work. If people just weren't so BLIND, they'd see that I belong to God, and they wouldn't treat me so badly, then I'd be able to be nicer to THEM. If people would just COOPERATE, I wouldn't HAVE to lose my temper. If my teacher wasn't such a bore, I'd be GETTING better grades. If my company would give me a much-deserved RAISE, I wouldn't BE so far in debt! What's WRONG with these people, anyway? If the people around me would just straighten UP, my life would be terrific."

I had started to believe that this wonderful existence that the Bible promises, was reserved for after we died. We had so many positive things to look forward to, now that we belonged to God, but my life just wasn't reflecting all those things, AND I had been told in churches that this was the reward we received when we got to Heaven. One day the Lord showed me something in a vision that changed my mind about that.

He showed me three distinct levels, as though He had drawn four straight lines across a paper, from left to right, with ample space between each line, creating three empty, rectangular spaces, stacked, each atop the other. As I watched, He began to fill in one of those spaces.

In the uppermost rectangle, where the word "Spirit" appeared, I saw myself walking steadily from the right to the left, and I was bathed in light. I was peaceful and happy, and had the impression that I was surrounded by love. Then words began to appear in that space around me as I walked. They were words like peace, harmony, love, satisfaction, confidence, trust, plenty, and joy. These words floated around me in this space, and accompanied my every step. Each step I took was sure and steady, and I appeared to be loving life in general. All good things surrounded me, which I understood by watching this image of myself. There was no fear whatsoever, for there was nothing there to fear. There was nothing in this place but me walking calmly on a well lighted path, surrounded by beautiful words which represented the things I was enjoying in this place. In this space, I was a happy, uncomplicated, trusting child. Just watching it made me long to be there.

I wanted my life to be like that, and I voiced this to the Lord. To my surprise, He said "You already have it." He told me that, within my spirit, I already possessed this magnificent, eternal life that He had given me. Then why didn't my REAL life reflect this, I wanted to know. He surprised me again by telling me that the life I was enjoying in this highest level WAS my real life. He said that my physical life was merely a REFLECTION. I did a quick mental inventory of my life, and decided God must have me mixed up with someone else today, because my life wasn't reflecting this beautiful place at all!

Then He began to fill in the lowest level in this vision, leaving the middle rectangle blank. In the lowest space, the word "Physical" appeared. On this lowest level, I watched myself walking in circles, and stumbling, and getting up and trying to walk again. I was covered in bruises and band aids from the journey so far. I would take a couple of steps, turn this way and that, and stop. I wasn't getting very far on this path, and it seemed like there was very little light, as though I were walking in a very dark shadow. Instead of light all around me this time, there were question marks in the space all around my head. This would have been an amusing sight, had it not been so pathetic, but I was definitely identifying with this lower level space. The Lord then informed me that this was the life I was reflecting in this world. Wow, I thought, what's wrong with THIS picture? I wanted to know how I could have this wonderful life that God had said He had already given me, in my spirit, and reflect such a mess in my physical life. If my physical life was really just a reflection, then why wasn't I reflecting the life from above?

It was only after I asked this question, that He began to fill in the middle space. The word "Soul" appeared within this space. I wasn't in this middle space. Slowly, one at a time, words began to appear in this rectangular area, between what I now understood to be my spirit life, and my physical life. Each word was enveloped by what appeared to be it's own separate cloud. The words that began to appear in these clouds were disturbing, such as anger, pain, humiliation, misunderstandings, wounds, religion, poverty, punishment, condemnation, rejection, betrayal, and many more. As each word appeared, they took up more and more space, until the space was completely filled with these bleak-looking clouds. The more clouds that appeared, the more they squeezed together, until they became like too many bodies stuffed into an elevator, squashing one another. I was all too familiar with each of these cloud-covered words. I had experienced them all.

What the Lord then told me was that THIS was the reason that there was such a difference between the eternal life that I already possessed, and what was being reflected in my physical life. There were too many things that my previous experiences had impacted on my soul, meaning my mind, will and emotions, and they were blocking the true life that God had intended for me, and not allowing it to be reflected. It just couldn't get through all those clouds. What a mess! This left me with a sense of hope-lessness, because how would I ever reflect what God had given me, when I had such a mess in the middle?

That day, God explained the prayer language to me in a different light. He showed me what appeared to be a golden shovel. He said that engaging in the power of the prayer language works like using a shovel, a tool that He had given me, to dig out, one by one, all the negative images that I had received from this world, in order to allow the life God had given me, to come through. He said we would now go after every wrong and distorted image that had been stored in me from the past, and remove them, allowing a true reflection of the life He had given me, to come through.

After seeing the vision of the levels of spirit, soul and body, I realized that I had been focusing in the wrong direction. I could see clearly now that it wasn't anyone else's fault that I wasn't experiencing the life God promised. It wasn't my fault, either, although the problem was in ME. Like so many others, my life experiences had caused all these negative images to be stored in me, and all of them created a barrier against experiencing God's gift of abundant life, in any other area than my spirit. I was either going to have to get rid of these wrong perceptions, or allow these CLOUDS to be the influence over my physical life. God had told me earlier, that we were energy, and I, like too many others, had had much too much negative impact on my energy field. When we're filled with negative impressions, each impression then becomes like a magnet, drawing negative situations to us, over and over.

The Bible says that when we see Him, we will become like Him. I had been led to believe that that meant when we got to Heaven, and saw Him face-to-face, we would somehow miraculously be transformed to be just like Him and, in my case, I only hoped I'd survive the shock of such a drastic transformation! I believed that, until the day came when God said to me "Look up SEE". That seemed silly to me because I thought everyone already KNEW what the word "see" means. However, when I looked it up, I came to find that to "see" means to perceive, or understand. As it turns out, that transformation process takes place here, little by little, each time we allow the Holy Spirit to escort us to God to "see" things as He sees them. Each time we "see" through His eyes, His understanding replaces our MIS-understanding, and in that area, we have become just like Him, for we automatically give up our misconceptions in the light of His more powerful truth.

I now understand that when the Bible says we have the mind of Christ, what's meant is that we have ACCESS to the mind of Christ, for this transformation. We didn't have to wait to die at all. We can have that here. All it takes is the power of the Holy Spirit, escorting us to God, to make the great exchange...our illusions, for His truth. Wouldn't we all rather see things as He sees them? Wouldn't we rather see people as God sees them? Wouldn't we rather be like HIM?

The transformation is a whole lot easier when we understand that it isn't the things on the OUTSIDE of us that we war against, and we need to overcome, but rather the things on the INSIDE of us. It's a much quicker process when we take our eyes off others around us, thinking that they're to blame. It isn't anyone else's fault if we're not able to reflect what God has given us. The culprit lies WITHIN.

This is the meaning of "working OUT our salvation". We work to clear out that cluttered soul, thus bringing the salvation that's already ours, OUT into our physical lives. Remember, the

Bible doesn't say that we're to work out the salvation of those AROUND us. That's THEIR job. Our job is to work out our OWN.

chapter 36
DOUBLE EXPOSURE

A lot of my healings have taken place over the years by God's super-imposing new pictures in my mind over the old negative picture that had been stamped there by the world around me. One example that made a tremendous difference in the way I felt about myself, was the day that God re-focused my vision concerning my birth.

I had been in quiet prayer, as usual. I saw a younger version of my mother standing before me, and she was pregnant with me, and smiling. I could see that it was nearly time for her to give birth to me. My dad was standing to the right of her, but a few feet away from her, and he looked like he was being punished. The vision made me feel bad, just like my childhood had. Slowly the vision was shifted, as though I had been looking through the lens of a camera, and as the lens shifted to the left, my mother was now the center of the vision, and my dad was no longer in the picture. I could now see my mother standing alone, and smiling.

I preferred the vision this way, although I had not been the one in charge of the re-focusing. It was sad to see her standing there though, awaiting my birth by herself. While I watched, an addition to the vision of my mother appeared, and my mother was no longer alone. Behind her, yet above her, over one shoulder, the Lord's face appeared, every bit as large as the image of my mother's entire body. He was very close to her, His face almost touching her, and He was looking at her with a tenderness in His eyes that told me she was cherished. He was beaming. I was given the impression that He was anxiously awaiting my birth, like a father would. I also was given the strong impression that He was very PLEASED that I was about to be born.

The reaction I had to this change of vision, was that I suddenly was convinced that I HAD been wanted. I was NOT an intrusion, but someone who's birth had been welcomed. This new shift of vision was a miracle in my life. A longing that I had always lived with, to know what it was like to be welcomed rather than just tolerated, had just been filled. It changed me inside. I felt the change. I came away from that vision with a new attitude about my birth. I felt finally, for the first time in my life, that my arrival in this world was not a tragedy, but a welcomed event. From that moment on, I never again felt guilty about being born, and now the child in me was smiling with a new-found acceptance. I belonged here, after all.

Some of us are exposed to things in life that leave negative imprints on our souls, concerning who we are. One of God's greatest gifts to us is His ability to superimpose a new imprint over the old, and cause us to see with new eyes....His eyes. If you've seen double exposure pictures, you know how deluding they can be. With a double exposure print on a roll of photo film, both images will show up on the same print, and cause confusion as to what the picture really is. They both become blurred because there are actually two pictures there. No matter what the second picture consists of, there's always the first imprint showing through, so neither print is interpreted clearly. That's why it's impossible for us to change ourselves. It takes God to make the changes. We might suppress, or subdue the old images inside, but God can completely wipe them out.

I had memorized scriptures concerning being accepted, but my belief in being accepted was always blurred. I'd read that repetition will put a thought from your conscious mind, clear down into the subconscious, but all the repetition in the world hadn't seemed to convince me of my worth. I had a scar so deep that normal methods just didn't seem to work. When God, through the supernatural power of the Holy Spirit praying, imposed a new print in my mind, He inserted it over the negative that I'd been carrying for years, and I was really changed. His camera focuses on the hidden things in our subconscious, and since His camera is so much more powerful, when HE imposes a new print over the old, it is so strong, and so lasting, that it completely obliterates the power of the old image. It isn't that I can't remember the old image, but it's now just a faint, powerless whisper in the presence of His new, powerful statement. I AM loved! I always WAS! I knew that now. That day my dad's impression of my birth was replaced by my Heavenly Father's, and I've never felt the pain of the rejection of a father since.

I hadn't felt that I was worth anything before, because I, like any other child, had looked for that validation in my parents' eyes. My father couldn't give me that, for he had too many problems of his own, and my mother, although she tried, couldn't either, for the same reason. I had grown up with both parents, feeling like an orphan. The day I quit being an orphan, was the day the Lord showed me in a picture, that I was worth a lot to Him. There is no photographer on Earth who can remake an image like He can. Why? Because He alone has supernatural equipment, that's why.

chapter 37
SAFE!

There were difficult times in my marriage, but God used those times to reveal Himself to me in many different aspects of His personality. He allowed me to meet Him in ways that would serve to strengthen and to heal me. One time in particular was used to allow me to meet Him as the protective Father that He is, and that I had always needed. This was another life-changing event, occurring deep within. This incident also occurred while my second husband was still drinking.

It was a particularly long and hard spree that my husband had been on this time. He'd been drinking heavily for the last few weeks, and he had become more and more dangerous to be around. We'd gone through times like this before, which was one of the reasons I had trouble understanding why God had always told me to stay. He had always gotten me through these bad times, but this time the bad time didn't seem to be ending, and by now I had gone from being nervous to being downright terrified. My husband stormed into the house one afternoon in a drunken stupor, and stood in the kitchen glaring at me through glazed and piercing eyes. I was looking into the eyes of something that was no longer my husband, but something very dangerous, and I knew it.

The rage that he had carried inside for years had been getting stronger with each day that he was drinking, but now it had completely taken over. I froze. I didn't move or speak. The eyes that were challenging me, were NOT my husband's eyes, but eyes of something deadly that was now controlling him. He stood there glaring, eyes blackened with that rage, and said with a sarcastic smirk "I want to kill something". And of course, since I was the "something "he was staring at, I knew we had reached a very dangerous point in this situation. Then he said "If you're here when I get back, you're dead." He turned and went back out the door.

I stood there frozen in time, until I heard his truck leave, then I collapsed onto a kitchen chair, crying out, "Lord, I HAVE to get out of here! I've had ENOUGH of this! I know you've told me to stay where I am, but I'm telling you right now, I can't do this any more. I'm terrified! If you still want me to stay here, you'd better show me something NOW to get me through, or I'm outta here!" I was desperately angry.

I allowed the Spirit to pray, while mentally I was planning my escape. Suddenly, in the spirit, I saw a tiny two-inch tall image of my husband standing on the corner of the table where I was sitting, while a huge hand, nearly as big as my head, appeared beside it, and in the same fashion that you would shoot a marble in a game, He flicked that image off the table into oblivion. At the very moment I saw this, I heard a firm, authority-filled voice say "He will not touch you, he will not harm you. If he even tries, I will annihilate him."

How can I describe the effect that had on me? A joy bubbled up from inside me, and I suddenly felt SAFE for the first time in my life. I had a FATHER who had just sworn to protect me! I had never before experienced anyone's protection from ANYTHING. I was in awe of this! It was such a powerful thing for me to think that someone would actually step in to keep me safe, that as soon as I saw and heard this, all of the terror that I'd been feeling, instantly disappeared, and I started to laugh . I absolutely KNEW that I was safe, for the first time ever, and it felt GOOD. I sat there a while, thanking God for who He was in my life, and then went back to complete whatever job I was in the midst of when this whole episode had started.

A half-hour later, my husband returned. When I heard him pull into the driveway, I calmly sat down at the table, facing the front door, not knowing what would happen next, but not afraid. All I knew was what God had said, and I was confident in that. When my husband entered the kitchen, he stopped right inside the door, and glared at me in all of the puffed-up fierceness that had terrified me earlier. Too late! I had already seen the size of my Father's hand, compared to him, and I knew he was no match for my "Dad". He started again with his murderous threat, but this time all I could see was that huge hand flicking that tiny man off the table, and the sight was so amusing now, that I started to laugh, right in the face of the enemy.

Then the strangest thing of all happened. The laughter seemed to startle him, and he began laughing, too! He was instantly back to being a normal person. It was over! The hateful thing that had been driving him, had vanished, and my husband actually looked relieved. I wasn't even upset with him now, for I knew that if this hadn't happened, I may have missed meeting my Father in a brand-new way. I still carry the knowledge of God's fierce protection toward me. I will always be in awe of that, and fiercely grateful.

Months later I watched a movie, in which a bear cub had been adopted by a powerful male grizzly, after the cub's mother had been killed. It's a beautiful movie, especially because of the end. Toward the end of the movie, the cub was alone and being threatened by a cougar, and the little cub had run for his life, but had gotten to a point where there was no place else to go. The cougar was operating in deadly cunning, and now he had the cub cornered. When he was within just a few feet of the cub, who had no way of escape, the whimpering cub suddenly stood straight up and faced his opponent, and roared in a combination of anger and despair. He stood up to the deadly cougar now in all of his little cub bravery, although you could see he didn't have a chance of survival. At that moment the roar of the cub became deafening, as the camera moved to show the huge male grizzly, who had heard his adopted baby's cries, and had come to stand behind him. This adoptive father was an awesome sight at that moment, standing fully erect, and towering over the cub in all of his powerful mass. That one, long, blaring threat from that magnificent grizzly took the cougars eyes from his intended victim, to the one who stood behind him. The cougar, knowing he was no match for the massive power of the adult, he swiftly retreated.

That's how God is with us. We are no match for the enemy on our own, but look out when "Daddy" arrives on the scene! We are safe, for there is nothing that can match His massive power, and there is nothing that will dare to try.

I've never advised anyone to stay in an abusive relationship for any reason, other than if God has specifically spoken to them to do so. Common sense tells you to get away from danger, and I had wanted to, but God had specifically asked me to stay where I was, so that's what I did. I couldn't understand why He would want me to stay in such a situation, but He had a plan, and that was to reveal more of HIMSELF to me as I obediently stayed. I may have hated my circumstances back then, but had I not had them, I don't think I ever would have come to know my Father in the way that I know Him now. I wouldn't trade that knowledge for ANYTHING, and I don't really mind now, how I came about getting it. If God hasn't specifically told you to remain in what appears to be a dangerous situation, then get out! The only reason I stayed was because God asked me to, even when I didn't understand. He never demanded, He just requested, and I loved Him too much to say no.

Do NOT think that because this happened to me, that you can assume the same thing would happen to you. People get killed in abusive situations every day. God doesn't ask all people to stay in something that threatening. All I'm talking about here is how He showed me His fatherly protection.

Remember what I said earlier. His spoken word to me is what I stand on, but it's for ME. Don't try to stand on MY word from God. All situations are different, as are the different plans for our lives. If you're in a difficult situation, don't assume anything. Go to God to get your instructions. Get your spoken word for YOU, and when you do, you can bet you can count on it!

What had appeared to be a life-threatening situation for me, God had used as a way to heal me in a way that I didn't even know I needed. I needed to know that my Father would protect me, and because of what He showed me, I now had a confidence I'd never known before. I wasn't "on my own" any more. I had a mighty and powerful companion and friend. I had a Father who really cared about me, and was strong enough to keep me safe.

chapter 38
"THE WORST IS YET TO COME"

I mentioned earlier that there had been a particularly difficult three-year period during which I wondered if I would survive at all, but this period had brought about some of the most dramatic instances of God revealing himself in the midst. I'm sure a lot of people would insist that "stay where you are" was NOT God's instruction, because, they would say, He wouldn't ASK any of His children to live in such adversity. But it's in adversity that we grow. He could have rescued me, but He honored the classroom that I had chosen, in order to allow me to experience what I needed. It was in the most difficult times that I got to know Him in a much more profound way than I otherwise would have.

God doesn't uncaringly put us into difficult situations. We put ourselves there because of the things we need to learn. God, who knows the desires of our hearts better than WE do, knows just how to bring about the fulfillment of those desires. I wanted to KNOW Him. It's one thing to read about His personality, His provision, and His promises in the Bible. It's another thing entirely, when you get to experience these things for yourself. I can read it and believe it, or I can live it and KNOW it.

Don't get me wrong here. I don't believe that anyone needs to deliberately go looking for trouble to live in, in order to get to know God. I didn't DELIBERATELY do that, either. What I DO mean is, if you're in a hard place, and God has instructed you to stay, it's only because He already knows He's going to take care of you in it. You're there because there's something you need to learn. He can use that very circumstance to introduce Himself, in all of the different aspects of His personality. He will also use it to change us and heal us, but He does NOT abandon us.

During that most difficult period of time, there was something even more powerful that He was going to teach me about, that I had not yet even HEARD of. When He did, I learned something so valuable about a problem that many women (and sometimes men) are caught in, and the reason that they can't seem to conquer because of it. This is how it started.

One evening, as Joyce and I sat at my kitchen table in prayer, the Lord made a statement to me that made me uneasy, to say the very least. He simply said "The worst is yet to come". This was shortly before we came to the end of the alcoholic era that had kept me so unnerved for so long. I couldn't imagine what He meant by this statement, because looking back over the insanity I'd already experienced, I wondered what could be worse than what had already been happening.

All hell had broken loose again, and I never knew from one day to the next what kind of subtle terror would be taking place in my life. When I asked Him what could possibly be worse than things that had already happened, He said "Stark Reality." We, of course, wanted to know what He meant by that statement too, but He now remained silent. We had no choice but to leave it at that, and wait. I knew from past experience, if He wouldn't tell me now, He WOULD tell me, or He would show me.

The following morning when I awoke and sat up in bed, it was as if I had just emerged from a drugged stupor. My mind was so clear, that I felt as though I had just awakened from a dream that had been going on for years. I looked around the room, startled by this new awareness, and suddenly realized that my life was a horror! I knew that before, but this time it was as though I were suddenly awakened to the REALITY of it. I was no longer observing my life from a passive detachment, but I was seeing the nightmare I had been living in for what it really was ...a nightmare.

Oh my God, I thought, this is REAL. This is really my LIFE. This is AWFUL! I was in touch with the reality of my own circumstances for the first time in YEARS. I was appalled at the mentally and emotionally abusive conditions I'd been living under. I couldn't believe all that had been happening to me, and that I hadn't been able to see it before. WHY hadn't I been able to SEE this? I now knew that, unless drastic steps were taken, it wasn't going to get better.

I got out of bed in amazement that morning. I couldn't believe that I'd been this mistreated, and had even THOUGHT that it was no big problem to live like this. I was so shocked by this awakening, that I couldn't even comprehend what had made me think my life was okay. It was then that the Lord's words came back to me. "Stark reality." No wonder He had said "the worst is yet to come". It was a horrible shock to see what my every-day home life consisted of. Why all the violence? Why all the name calling? Why all the accusations? Why all the insanity? A myriad of questions rushed to the forefront of my mind. Then the biggest question of all arose from deep within. Why had I ever put up with this in the first place? Why had it not been REAL to me until now?

This was the question I presented to the Lord that morning. What had been wrong with me, that I couldn't see this for what it was before? Why had I sat in such a daze, thinking things would somehow be all right? Why, in this stupor, had I thought my circumstances would improve? God, no wonder people thought I was crazy for living in this alcoholic mess, and always being the victim. WHY had I thought it didn't matter? Now that I was seeing my circumstances clearly for the first time in years, I couldn't believe it myself! What had been WRONG with me, I wanted to know. I had already learned why I had gotten into this type of relationship in the first place, but now I was seeing the ridiculousness of the situation still going on, and THIS time with a clear mind.

God, always faithful, had opened up a really large can of worms this time. And in His faithfulness, He answered me. "Trauma" was the next word He gave me. Of course I didn't know what He meant by this, so I immediately headed for the dictionary to find out whatever I could about trauma. Then He began to explain. What He told me that day would change my opinion concerning myself and other women in these circumstances forever, and hopefully it will give you some insight into the real problem, too.

He began to explain trauma to me, and how it works, in a way that I could understand. He reminded me of an automobile accident that I'd been in years before. My car had been hit by an eighteen-wheeler, and totaled. The truck driver had said later, that I should have been killed, but I had walked away from the accident, stunned, but functioning. I wasn't even really concerned that this had happened. I just went home without a car. It wasn't any more upsetting to me, than if I'd experienced the wreck in a dream.

It was a day and a half later, when I was talking with some people about something else, when suddenly I felt an invisible weight lift from me, and just as suddenly, the realization of the accident became REAL. I started sobbing, "Oh, my God, I wrecked the car! Oh, MY GOD, I wrecked the car!" I was now dealing with all of the horror of the accident. Until the moment that the shock that I was in, wore off, I had been aware of the wreck, but hadn't been in touch with the REALITY of it. I hadn't been upset, I hadn't been scared, and I hadn't felt any pain.

He explained to me that emotional and psychological trauma occurs in the same way that shock takes over in physical distress. Any time we experience something that we cannot comprehend, because it is too painful for our minds or emotions to handle, trauma takes over to numb us from the pain of the incident. It works in the same order as shock does when we're in an accident. When physical pain is too great, we enter into a state of shock, much like entering into a dream state, as though it never really happened. At that time, since we can't get in touch with the reality, we don't feel the pain. We won't feel the pain until the shock wears off.

When we take a mental or emotional "blow" that is much too painful for our minds or spirits to tolerate, we enter into a state of mental or emotional trauma which dulls that pain, so we can survive it, and carry on. We become stunned by the blow, and although we've been emotionally or psychologically wounded, it becomes, for the sake of survival, a dream...something that we tell ourselves didn't really happen, although we know it really did.

In order to be able to function in other areas, we detach from the incident that could cause that much pain, while trauma energy serves as a buffer against the impact. Trauma energy works like a pain-killing drug in these situations, keeping safe our sanity.

However, while it remains, it also keeps us from getting in touch with the very reality we need concerning the incident that caused the pain in the first place. If we can't feel the pain, we don't deal with the cause of it, but to feel the pain would hurt too much, so we don't touch it, mentally or emotionally. We set it aside, for it is much too painful to deal with right now.

What had happened to me, the Lord was explaining to me now, was what has happened to so many of His children. So many have been mentally or emotionally traumatized in childhood, then over and over again. By the time the first trauma energy is about to wear off, another unbearable mental or emotional blow is inflicted, and a whole new trauma energy takes over. Trauma after trauma taking place over the years, causes the victim to live in a veritable "dream state", unable to get in touch with their true emotions, or thoughts. Others wonder how we ever made such horrible choices for ourselves, but horrible choices never bothered us, for in that "dream state", nothing is really real anyway. It's as if we're being drugged over and over again by these incidents, which are keeping our minds and emotions sedated. A state of trauma acts like an emotional or mental morphine.

People get very upset about the abusive circumstances some of us live in, and they get angry because we can't seem to see how bad things are, but since trauma victims aren't in touch with their own pain, they just can't see what all the fuss is about. And even if they DO understand what the fuss is all about, there's another problem that the trauma victim faces.

Trauma is a PARALYZING agent. No wonder a trauma victim can't think how to escape the circumstances. First of all, when it isn't real, what's to escape? Secondly, when the trauma victim becomes aware of the need for escape, they don't seem to have the ability to follow through. You see, trauma scars the psyche. In other words, it scars the mind, causing rational thoughts to be blocked and unable to be acted upon. That, I found out, is one of the major reasons that a person isn't able to easily walk out on an abusive situation. These people aren't idiots. There are many intelligent people who have lived, and ARE living, in very unhealthy relationships. They may KNOW they need to get away from abuse, but the paralyzing agent of trauma, makes them unable to do so.

The fact WAS, trauma had been a culprit in my life for years, and trauma was what I'd needed to learn about. What I came to find out was that my mind and emotions had been so sedated by traumas, that I didn't find it a problem to function under these circumstances. The only thing that had allowed me to function though, was the fact that I WAS in a state of trauma, which kept me numbed. I didn't know the difference, however, until the trauma energy was removed, and I could see clearly. A state of trauma is a blissful escape from reality, if reality is just too hard to bear, but we don't want to remain in this drugged stupor any longer than we have to. Trauma energy, like any other drug, must be removed. Then, and only then, can real progress toward complete inner healing begin to be made.

God did have a plan for me though, that would be better than just escaping to another prison, and another traumatizing relationship, and that was to continue to heal me inwardly in my current circumstances, until I'd be able to overcome everything in me that had allowed me to accept an abusive lifestyle in the first place. He also, in His all-knowing, knew that the reward for my staying and being healed from the inside out, was that, as I became more positive and stronger, I would no longer draw this type of behavior to me. He was enabling me to become strong enough to take the target off my mind and emotions that had drawn the bullets every time.

When God said to me "Stark Reality", He was going to allow me to see the reality of my life by removing all the trauma energy that I lived in. Now I would be able to get in touch with my own feelings. That was the beginning of even more healings to come. The beauty of this is that we can all ask to have trauma energy removed, and He is able to do this for us, so we can walk out of the dream state, and into a better life. Joyce and I have been able to pray about trauma energy and its effects on others, many times since learning about this from the One who is able to remove it. I think all people have experienced mental and emotional shock to some degree, but if it's slight, the victim can readily walk away from a situation that would traumatize. That's why some people will run from an abusive person upon first contact. The ones who have a difficult time walking away are those who have been deeply traumatized, and been more or less paralyzed by it. Having trauma energy removed is the same as being freed from any other drug. Now we must learn how to deal with life in a different way.

For years I've heard people make really unkind and uninformed statements about women who have been unable to get away from abusive relationships. The most ridiculous of all is the statement that these women must like being treated that way, or they'd leave. There is no such thing as a human being who would choose to be abused over being loved, but keep in mind that these women are dealing with that paralyzing agent called trauma. The more traumatized they are, the more we need to love them. A lot of positive love energy can help keep them balanced while they grow stronger. Most times we just walk away from these people, disgusted, thinking they have the same ability as anyone else to walk away from that hell, but they don't. PRAY for them that God removes this force from their lives, so they CAN move out of that paralyzed state, and get on with the business of confronting their situations, so they, too, can begin living rather than just surviving.

The worst thing we can do to a traumatized person is ask them to take the same action any normal, rational, un-wounded person would take. Try loving them instead, and understanding that they can't get in touch with the rational thinking they NEED until the trauma energy is displaced. To yell at, and be disgusted with, a traumatized person is as lame as kicking someone who's just crawled away from a car wreck., battered and bleeding. Gentleness is needed at a time like that, not MORE abuse!

God removed trauma energy from me, and He can do It for anyone. Abused people need someone to go to God on their behalf, for they are so mentally and emotionally sedated that they have no idea what to do. I know. I was there. I lived it. I had the privilege of a steadfast prayer partner to pray this through with me. It's amazing the things we find out when we're dedicated to time spent with God, and when we allow Him to lead the way through the sickening maze.

The problem with a child being introduced to painful experiences, is that the painful experiences usher the dream state into their lives very early. Unfortunately, if the painful circumstances aren't corrected, and trauma after trauma occurs, it serves to seal the child into that detached state, where he or she learns to accept this psychologically and emotionally drugged condition as a way of life.

I've read about people who are considered "crisis-oriented", and I know now that I was one of those people. They've lived through shock after shock while they were growing up, and they will actually bring about one crisis after another throughout their adult lives. I don't know if they want the rush of adrenalin that courses through their bodies during the crisis itself, as I have read. That could be true, but I also believe now that a state of trauma can become as addicting as any other drug of choice, and it has become my opinion that there are some crisis-oriented people who will unknowingly bring about another crisis just because the dream state is wearing off. They need another "fix" in order to remain in that blissful state of unreality that they have become accustomed to. After all, if the trauma is permitted to wear off, we're going to find ourselves subject to a lot of pain from a lot of lousy circumstances, so better to remain numbed by trauma, than be made to face years of painful memories with no way to deal with them.

In order to remain numbed, they must have a crisis first in order for the "dream state" to keep taking over. Another crisis is a small price to pay if you've become addicted to the mental and emotional sedative called trauma. This is by no means a deliberate act on the part of the one sedated, simply a familiar and automatic way of escape.

I had considered myself to be a strong person. I even marveled at my own ability to endure harsh circumstances, and still go on. I had a habit of jokingly telling others that if they needed someone to unload their burdens on, they could unload them on me, because I was tough and could handle ANYTHING. At least that's the way I saw it, until the Lord informed me that I had been lying to my friends. I was shocked to hear this, because I had always said that my problem was that I couldn't tell a decent lie, not even to save my own neck , and I would certainly never CONSIDER lying to my friends. Now I had to find out what God thought I had lied about. He informed me that I was lying every time I told my friends I was tough and could handle ANYTHING, and that the truth was, I had NOT been handling anything at all. I argued that I had handled MUCH in the past few years.

He very gently informed me now, that no, I hadn't handled any of the things that had been happening. All I had done was allow those things to drive me deeper and deeper inside myself to hide again from another abusive situation. He wanted me to be able to handle life now, He told me, and all the while I thought that's what I'd been doing. I had to admit, once He told me this, that He was right. I hadn't been handling my life, I'd just been enduring it. Boy, the lies we tell ourselves!

There's only one who can remove the power of painful memories, and the trauma that keeps us quiet while these memories eat away at us, and that's God Himself. He can and will bring about a much-needed permanent healing from the wounds that introduced you to that sedated lifestyle in the first place. He alone knows what path you need to take to get you to your healing. Whether He Himself reveals things to you to set you free, or leads you to others who can help you in these areas of inner healing, it doesn't matter. The important thing is for you to realize the problem is there, and ask Him to fix it. He'll take it from there, and I assure you, He is very good at what He does.

chapter 39
RIPPLES IN THE POOL

Have you ever stood overlooking a lake so tranquil that it appeared to be made of glass? If you haven't, you've probably at least seen a picture of a lake like that. Behind the lake stands the most majestic, snow-topped mountain you've ever seen. At the base of the mountain is a lush, grassy field that slopes downward, stopping just short of the water's edge A multitude of great, tall evergreen trees stand at attention on either side of that scene, also skirting the edge of the water. The trees extend to the outer edges of your vision. A clear blue sky rests gently over the entire area. This breathtaking beauty is doubled by the reflection in the mirror-like lake. The water is so still, and the reflection is so perfect, that it's hard to tell where one ends and the other begins.

You can become so caught up in the exact-likeness reflection, that you can forget that it's only a reflection, and can easily mistake it for the real thing. This is the scene that appeared to me in a vision that God showed me to help me further understand where changes are made.

The day this vision appeared, I sat in awe of the beauty of it. As I watched, my attention was drawn downward to a gentle movement that had just been added to the scene. The movement was that of a dove, gliding gracefully across the sky. There IS nothing more peaceful than this, I thought, as I watched the dove slowly glide across the wide expanse. Then another movement caught my attention. From the same area from which the dove had appeared, a hawk had just entered the scene, making his way toward the dove. He was flying faster than the dove, as if to overtake him, and I suddenly realized the dove was in grave danger. Becoming alarmed for the unsuspecting dove, I whispered "Lord, please don't let the dove be killed."

The Lord answered me and said, "Remove the hawk from the scene.

Seeing the hawk getting closer to the dove, I instinctively reached out to pluck the hawk from the scene, and to my surprise ripples began forming in the sky, widening and multiplying. Startled, I realized that I hadn't touched the hawk at all. I had only touched the reflection of the hawk. Quickly, I looked up in the vision to the real sky above, only to find the REAL hawk now dangerously close to the dove. The scene faded, as my heart sank, knowing that I hadn't helped at all. The reflection had been so clear, that I hadn't even realized that it was only the reflection I'd been looking at.

It was then that the Lord began to talk to me about what he had just shown me. He told me that everything that I saw around me in this physical world was simply a reflection of things that were happening in the unseen realm of the spirit. We only see reflections, though, because that's all we can see with the physical eyes. Unfortunately, we don't know to look to another realm to do something about a problem. We think the problem is in this physical world, so this is where we focus our attention, and this is where we focus our prayer. He told me that day, that when it came to removing problems, we must go to this higher realm to change them, for that is where the problem originates. Otherwise, we are just touching the reflection, making ripples in the pool.

The interesting thing about making ripples in the pool, is that the ripples distort the scene, causing us to ASSUME a problem is gone, simply because we can't see it momentarily because of the distortion. We've prayed, and we've made our ripples, so we think the problem has been solved. We now relax back into peace, only to be completely shocked to find the problem still exists, and here it comes again! What we didn't understand was that we had only disturbed a reflection, and although we couldn't see the problem for the moment, we haven't removed it where it really existed, so as soon as the water stills again, the problem will be reflected again.

The Bible says that God's thoughts are higher than our thoughts, and His ways are higher than our ways. That simply means He sees from a higher advantage, so He sees the ENTIRE situation, while we're limited to seeing just what's evidenced in the physical, the reflections. The impending danger that I had been shown was an accurate account of what was happening above. It was accurate because of the stillness of the water. All too often, the winds of adversity come into our lives, disturbing our peace, and thus disturbing our peaceful waters. The wind causes ripples and waves on the surface of the water. We may be aware that there's a problem, but if we aren't peaceful and serene, which we usually aren't in the midst of a problem, we may be seeing a distorted image of what is actually causing it. Now we'll pray concerning what the problem APPEARS to be, due to the distortion of the image, while we allow the true cause of the problem to still exist to be reflected again.

When the wind of adversity comes, we need the power of the Holy Spirit to guide us to a higher place, above where that emotional wind blows, distorting images. We allow the Holy Spirit within us to pray in His own language, escorting us to God's higher level, where we can see the situation as God sees it, and we can pray accordingly. Then, and only then, can we be assured that the work has been done that was needed.

If we're going to believe what the Bible says, then we need to believe ALL of it. To say that the Bible is God's Word, and truth, and then ignore the Holy Spirit's power that is available to us, by ignoring everything written about the Baptism of the Holy Spirit, and the power available to a child of God through it, just simply makes no sense. Read it again. It's there. And it's real. And, it's available to you. You do not have to sit by helplessly any longer, always wondering why your life is in turmoil.

I've heard nightmare stories as to what people have been taught concerning the Baptism of the Spirit, and the gifts of the Spirit, and "speaking in tongues", and it's amazing to me how many wonderful children of God have been duped into believing that this power was done away with, or that it's something evil, and to be feared. It's sad, really, for they've been made, by men's teachings, to be non-believers. They've been kept from having all that God has for them by these fear-filled interpretations.

The KJV Bible mentions in I Corinthians 13:10, "When that which is perfect is come, then that which is in part shall be done away...", and some have led people to believe that that meant when Jesus came, for He was the perfection they were waiting for, that there was no further need for the "special gifts". How could that be, when Jesus, being perfect, is the one who sent the Holy Spirit, who imparts these gifts? Has it occurred to anyone that the perfection that the Bible was referring to could be a perfect reflection of Jesus IN US?

I Corinth 13:10, in the Living Bible translation says, " But when we have been made perfect and complete, THEN the need for these inadequate special gifts will come to an end, and they will disappear. If we've not yet been able to reflect the perfect and completely loving nature of God, then it stands to reason that we still have need of the spiritual tools to get the clutter of this world out of us, so we CAN reflect His love properly. Do we still carry restrictions as to what type of people we're able to love?

In the beginning of the new covenant with God, when the Church was forming, everyone who believed was given the Gift of God, the Holy Spirit, and began speaking in languages that they did not know, which was the evidence of that gift. Has God stopped giving these gifts to His children? No, He's never stopped giving the gift of the Spirit to His kids. But remember, the Gift of God was given to them that BELIEVED. But how are they to operate in a gift from Him if they're taught that they're not supposed to have it? Or worse yet, taught that the very power of God resident within them is something to be feared.

I used to wonder where that power came from, myself, until I found out that it wasn't something that mysteriously came through the air and washed all over you, baptizing you in this power. What I found out was that, at the very moment that Jesus is invited into our lives, the Holy Spirit joins together with our spirit, which was dead to God, and brings our spirit back to life. At that moment, when the Holy Spirit takes up residence in us, we ALREADY carry all the power that He possesses. He doesn't

SHED His power just to come and live in us, He brings it WITH Him. So receiving the power of the Holy Spirit isn't the problem... we've already got it! The problem is getting past everything we've been taught against it, which keeps the Holy Spirit restricted in us. We need to get rid of those restrictions, allowing the power that we already carry to be released. It has to flow! And it will flow, right out of your mouth, in words you don't understand with your own mind, but God does.

So what's to fear? You've carried that very power within you, since you met the Lord. It hasn't hurt you so far, has it? Well, it hasn't hurt you, but it can't help you either, if it never gets out of the holding tank!

chapter 40
OPENING THE TANK

You've invited the Lord to take over your land (your life), because it has become parched and dry, and nothing seems to grow on your land, but weeds, i.e., problems. You've met people who have beautiful gardens, and they told you that their beautiful gardens began to grow when they asked Jesus to take over their land, so you decided to give Him your land, too.

When the Lord took over your land, the first thing He did was install, right smack in the middle of your property, deep in the ground, a great, huge tank filled with the purest sparkling water that He had brought to you from Heaven. You plant all sorts of flower seeds, (truths) and others come by and share their seeds with you, too, so you wait for your garden to blossom. What you're waiting for is these truths to be manifested in your life, but the change you expected hasn't come.

The people with the beautiful gardens had assured you that letting Jesus take over your property would result in you having a beautiful garden, too, but you're thinking by now that they lied to you, for your property (your life) hasn't really changed. It's still parched and dry and barren, except for the weeds. You decide that maybe having a garden like that was not what Jesus wanted for your property. Maybe the flowers are only for a select few. Wrong! He supplies us all with everything we need to live an abundant life. What, then, is the problem?

The tank that holds the water to make your flowers grow has been installed, but never opened. Since the tank was deep inside the ground, nobody knew it was there but God, and since it was hidden, you didn't even think about it, let alone realize the importance of it.

A neighbor comes by, and notices that you still have a property full of weeds, and upon seeing that you have no flowers growing, he asks why you didn't give your property to the Lord, like the others had. You inform him that you did, but you must not be supposed to have the flowers, because the flowers never grew. The neighbor understands the problem immediately, and asks if he can use his shovel to go digging on your property. You figure it can't hurt anything, since the property looks so bad anyway, so you give permission for him to dig.

He doesn't have to dig long until he reaches his destination. He has touched the tank! He moves quickly to unplug a pipe, and water begins to release from the tank at a nice, steady pace. He fills in the hole he had dug, and now it doesn't really look like anything is happening again, because it's all underground. But as days go by, and the water keeps flowing under the ground, the ground is becoming moist, even to the top. This moisture is saturating the ground, you notice, from deep down inside. As this steady saturation continues, you soon find little starts of plants beginning to sprout up from the ground. Your seeds are opening! They're starting to grow!

You're thrilled at the prospect of actually having a beautiful garden, too, but then you look at all those weeds, and decide they need to go, for they would be an eyesore in your garden. You've tried to pull the weeds before, only to find that you couldn't break the roots loose from that dry, parched ground. Saddened, you walk over to one of those weeds, and halfheartedly pull at it, knowing that they never would come out before, no matter how hard you tried. But this time is different. It's like a miracle, how easily that weed came out, when you didn't expect it to! The water , you now realize, laughing, has softened the earth to such a degree that the roots of the weeds can finally let go.

This is the power that you carry inside when you give your land, which is YOU, over to the Lord. He installs the Holy Spirit, the water tank, to bring about abundance in your life, and to help to remove the weeds. The prayer language that the Spirit uses to flow through you is the water of life. Don't fall for the lie that abundance is for a select few! Don't permit yourself to be cheated out of using what you already possess. Remember, you have the same pure water tank in you that God gives to all of His children. Don't let anyone keep you from having it opened. Not only will you get the weeds out, but your land (your life) will become like a Garden of Eden, full of all good things, and the fragrance of God's truth, matured in you, will attract many. And when they ask how you came about having such a beautiful garden, when their land is still full of weeds, you will be able to let them know how it happened. You'll not forget to tell them about the tank. If their tank is plugged, and the pure water of the Holy Spirit isn't flowing, you can always use your shovel…your spirit prayer …to unplug their pipes, too.

Are you wondering what it is that keeps the pipe plugged? There are many things that can stop the flow of the power of the Spirit within, such as fear of the unknown, doubt that you could have this, and unbelief that it is for God's kids in our day. And where does this fear, doubt, and unbelief come from? From us listening to what un-enlightened men say about the Scriptures, rather than reading the Bible and just believing it, or from others telling us that that power died out with the disciples, but how could that have happened yet, since we ourselves are disciples of Christ!

I'll guarantee you that, as long as there's a disciple of Christ in this world, the gifts of the spirit will not die. We have a super-natural Father, who gives supernatural gifts to His kids. It would not be a loving Father who would just select a few of His children to give this gift to, when it's the very power that we need in order to be the overcomers that the Bible says we are. Since He's no respecter of persons, He gives the gift of the Holy Spirit to ALL of His children, and the only requirement for using what He's given, is to BELIEVE.

chapter 41
PLAYING THE GAME

I've heard a lot of Christians say that they don't have much time for prayer or Bible reading because of all the things they have to do in a day. The problem with being too busy is that the "busy-ness", creates a spiritual dilemma. We can get so busy that we starve our spirits for daily nourishment. I've always enjoyed housework, but let's face it, it can become drudgery when it's the same things to do day in and day out. I stumbled across a formula years ago that would not only take the drudgery out of housework, but made it more fun than I had ever imagined. I called it "playing the game".

This game worked well for me, to bring about a balance and a self-discipline to my life. I have a tendency to take hold of whatever project I begin with the determination of a pit bull. I find it difficult to let go until the project has been completed. I can't tell you how many times over the years my daughter has grinned at me, with one eyebrow raised in her typical Sherlock Holmes, mystery-solving style, and said " Gee, Mom, hmmmm....could it possibly BE... that you might be just a tiny bit compulsive?"

And that's how my daughter laughingly describes me. I actually worried about that for a while, until someone else said that I wasn't compulsive at all, but simply did whatever I did with my whole heart. I've got to admit that I liked that explanation MUCH better, so that's the one I accepted. My daughter always said it jokingly, with no criticism intended, but I sometimes wonder how many wonderful people have been labeled "compulsive", when all the've really been is "wholehearted", but have simply not known how to direct that wholehearted energy in the right direction.

When I'd read my Bible, or a book, I'd want to read on and on and on, but there was work to be done. If I got up in the morning and started cleaning, or started working on a project, reading had to be set aside until the work or project was finished. The game I discovered, that brought about the balance, was to "read a chapter, do a job".

I discovered that if I limited myself to ONE chapter in my Bible, then performed ONE household chore, I got more work done in a day than most, and at the same time, I read so much Bible that I was always on top of things. The game consisted of ...read one chapter, then make my bed. Read another chapter, then dust the furniture, in that room only. Read another chapter, and run the sweeper in that room. Three chapters were being digested while one room was now finished. Now I'd move on to the bathroom. Read a chapter, clean the bathtub. Read a chapter, clean the sink and vanity area, read a chapter, clean the toilet, read a chapter, sweep the bathroom, another chapter, scrub the bathroom floor. Now it would be time to move on to the next room.

All the time that I'd be doing whatever job had become the "pause" between chapters, I'd be digesting what I'd just read. Eight chapters read, and two rooms finished! I loved playing this game. I became once again a child playing for the day. My house was in order, I was continuously learning, and I was always in a great mood.

I'd been doing this for weeks, not having any idea of the value of this "game", other than entertaining myself, until one day when a woman I'd met in a Christian meeting called. We talked for a while, when suddenly she wanted to know how it was that I was in SUCH a great mood. I was startled by the question, because at the time I hadn't realized how much more positive my mood had become. She informed me that she'd been pretty down for a while because of things going on in her life, and wanted to know what I was doing to keep myself so "up". I told her that I wasn't doing anything in particular to be in such a good mood, but then I thought of the game I'd been playing. I told her about the game I had invented , wondering if this might have something to do with my mood, and she was shocked. She said that she'd never heard of anyone doing their daily routine that way, but after listening to the positive mood I was in, she was going to try it herself!

She left that phone conversation that day with an excitement about playing a game that I hadn't considered anything more than a way to keep myself from boredom. I left the conversation that day with a whole new awareness of the value of the game.

There were times when the game would be put "on hold" for a while, maybe minutes, maybe an hour, while God would explain more to me concerning things that I'd been reading, but other than that, my routine went on happily, as usual.

If "the game" sounds like it would take too much time in a day to keep running back to read a chapter, try it once and see what happens. My daily work seemed to be done in less time than usual, leaving me plenty of time for extra projects that I never seemed to be able to get to before. And the spiritual growth that took place during that time was phenomenal. There was NEVER any room for boredom, or for negative thoughts, for I was digesting spiritual food all day long. The greatest reward was the communion time with God that this game led me into time after time.

chapter 42
HOME BEFORE DARK

Early one afternoon, when I had been playing the game, I had worked my way through the house and was finishing now in the kitchen. The words "Home before dark" appeared in front of my face, lingering in the air for a moment, then faded, only to return again minutes later. When the phrase appeared the second time, I sat down at the kitchen table to ask the Lord what those words were about.

He began His conversation with, "It's like this. Let's say you have two children."

"I Do have two children." I was now an interested student, talking to my teacher.

"Let's say that your son is eighteen, and your daughter is three." He had definitely changed the ages of my kids for the sake of the lesson.

"Okay, Lord, let's say that." I agreed.

"Your son has been with you for eighteen years, and you've taught him continuously through these years. He has grown to be a strong, muscular, wise young man," He continued. "Let's say he approaches you one day and tells you that he wants to walk across town to see a friend, and says that he'll be back sometime after dark. Would you let him go?"

I didn't hesitate to answer. I said "Sure, why not?"

"Exactly," He affirmed. "There would be no reason to object. You know that he is able to handle himself in any situation that might come up, and you also know that if he got into a situation that he couldn't handle, that he has the wisdom to call home immediately for advice or help."

I agreed, and He went on. "Now let's say that your three year old daughter tells you she is going to walk across town to HER friend's house, and that she, too, will return after dark. Would you let her go?"

Laughing at such a ridiculous thought, I chuckled, "Not a chance!

"Why wouldn't you?" He surprised me with this question.

"Why WOULD I?" I exclaimed. "She'd be too little, she'd get lost, she doesn't know how to defend herself, and ANYTHING could happen to her out there. She'd be HELPLESS!" I was wondering by now where this conversation was headed.

"Then you wouldn't allow her to go to play with her friend?" He questioned.

"Yes, she could go see her friend, but I wouldn't let her WALK there. I would take her myself, and I'd go and get her again, and bring her home BEFORE dark. Then I'd know she was safe." I expressed a simple logic.

He now surprised me with His next statement. "I'm like that with my children, too."

"What do you mean, Lord?" I didn't understand how this applied.

"I have children who've been with me for many years, for various reasons, they've not been able to grow. They are like your three-year-old, still too inexperienced, and too weak to be able to have the freedom that my more mature children have grown into. I watch over them carefully to protect them. There is a dark time coming upon the world, but do not fear for my little ones. I love them, and I will keep them safe. I will not allow the darkness to overtake them. I will bring them home with me before I would let that to happen. I will not lose them to the darkness."

It was at this moment that I realized the incredibly strong parental love that our Father has for all of us. Not only is He the strong one, the one that we can depend on to meet our every need, but He loves us also with a protective love that would scoop us away with Him to safety, rather than allow us to become lost in the darkness. I hadn't thought that I could love Him any more than what I already did, but after what He had just explained to me, I felt as though another chamber of my heart had just opened up to hold an even greater perception of His personality.

I was so impressed with His tender way of looking at us, with the same compassionate wisdom and delight with which we would view our own children, that I relaxed into this understanding with even more confidence than before that He knows best, and all He has for us is love.

He had said that there was a darkness coming, and I now thought to ask about that. He told me that yes, there was a dark time coming, but to just continue to develop my relationship with Him, and He would direct my every step. He said it would be a difficult time, but if His children would draw very close to Him, and learn and grow strong, He would direct us all , and we would make it safely through. While He was telling me this, I saw Him leading me by the hand, escorting me through what appeared to be a field of land mines. When He moved, I moved. When He stopped, I stopped. When He turned, I did the same. We moved in unison.

I promised I would try to remain that close to Him, but not trusting myself entirely, I also asked that He see to it that I remained close. I decided that asking for help in this area wasn't a bad idea at all.

He also told me that day that I would see, before the darkness fully came, what others would call premature deaths, but I was to trust in His wisdom, for He alone knew who would stay, and whom he would bring home with Him for their safety. I then understood that what I would have called a tragedy for a child of God, was simply a loving Father gathering His young ones into the protection of His arms.

chapter 43
BRIDLING A BLABBERMOUTH

Months later, I attended a meeting for the women's organization I belonged to. I had been working with this organization for three or four years now, and this meeting was the one that we held in preparation for the monthly gathering. At the end of the meeting, one of the other board members asked for prayer for a friend who, she said, was dying. He was only in his fifties, she informed us, and she stated that the Bible gives us seventy years, and she said he was being robbed.

Having been made aware of "Home before dark", after we prayed for him, I shared with her what God had told me about bringing his people home. She looked at me as though I were insane, and it was dropped. I cringed under the look on her face, and I decided at that moment that I'd never make THAT mistake again, but I would keep the information God gave me to myself, and only share with my closest prayer partners the things that God would tell me.

A couple of months later, when we were having our monthly meeting, the speaker began to tell the story of her own son's death. She talked about the heartbreak that she had gone through, and that if it hadn't been for God in her life, she hadn't known how she would have gotten through it at all. Every now and then, while she was talking, the Lord would say to me "Tell her about 'home before dark'."

Gripped by a silent panic, I responded each time with "I can't!"

I had already been judged as a lunatic for sharing that story with someone once, and I didn't think I could get past the humiliation of that experience to do it again. He gently persisted, until I finally told Him that the only way I could do this, would be if He would separate her from the other people there, at some point after the meeting, and I could tell only HER. That way, I figured, if I was going to look like an idiot again, it would be better to look like an idiot to just one person, as opposed to an entire roomful. I also figured I would be 'off the hook', and not have to actually do this because there really never was a time when guest speakers were alone in that room. I knew that already, from the years of being involved. Each monthly speaker was the designated celebrity for the day, and you never found them without someone talking to them about something. Yep, I was pretty safe, as far as I was concerned. No more embarrassing moments for me!

When the meeting was over, and people were praying with one another, or quietly discussing what the speaker had said, I kept my eye on the speaker, mostly to reassure myself that she wasn't alone, and making sure I wouldn't have to talk to her about something that I had had such a bad reaction to before. Assured that I was safe from having to humiliate myself, I entered into a whisper of a conversation with a lady standing near me, while I gathered up my Bible and my notebook and my purse.

I was just about ready to leave, when the Lord calmly said to me "Tell her now." Snapping to attention, I turned to see where the speaker was, and sure enough, she was now on the other side of the room, getting things together to leave, and there was no one anywhere near her. Wow! He was really going to make me DO this! I dreaded sharing this story again, because of the last time, but I had no choice, since I could see that my stipulation had been met, so I braced myself, and walked over to stand in front of her.

"Could I talk to you about something?" I asked. Of course she said "Yes", and despite my nervousness, I began to tell her the story about "home before dark".

As I stood there conveying everything He had told me, I was surprised to find, instead of a look of horror on her face, she was slowly nodding, and listening to every word. When I finished, she wiped tears from her eyes, and hugged me. She kept saying "Thank You, Lord...Thank You, Lord." Now THIS was not the reaction I had been expecting at all, and I was a little confused by it all. The only thing I knew was that she was thanking the Lord, so I thought this might not be a total disaster.

As I stood there with her, she explained to me what had just taken place. She said that, in her grief over her son's death, she had cried out to God to understand WHY! Her son was only twenty years old and had loved the Lord so much, that she couldn't understand why he had been taken. Then she said that what I had just told her, was exactly what the Lord had told HER in her time of greatest pain. The Lord had told her that something that only He knew about, would have taken place that would have devastated her son, and he would have, in that devastation, walked away from Him. He wouldn't have been strong enough to tolerate it. He had told her, she said, that the Lord had brought him home with Him to keep him safe.

She had already been told about "home before dark", but she had never been able to tell anyone about this, and sometimes she would doubt what she had heard. She then told me that, before coming to speak at this meeting, she had asked the Lord for a special comfort today concerning the loss of her son, because this was an especially difficult day for her. Today was the first anniversary of her son's death. She said that she hadn't even known if she'd be able to get through it, but she had come in obedience to him, trusting God for the comfort that she needed. He had sent me to confirm His spoken word to her.

With another long, strong hug, and an even stronger spirit experience for both of us, we parted ways that day, although not really. There would always be a bond between us now, whether we'd ever see each other again or not in this world. The bonds between the children of God are eternal, from everlasting to everlasting. And now that the "home before dark" story had been confirmed to both of us, I had a deeper understanding of Jesus' words in John 6:39 (Living Bible), "…that I should not lose even one of all those he has given me…". He meant that with all of His heart.

I have to say here that I had made a mistake telling the other lady about "home before dark", and that's why I had gotten such a bad reaction from her. God had not asked me to tell her. I had taken it upon myself to share that with her. She was not ready to hear it. I think a lot of times we make the mistake of telling people things that God has shown us, when they're not ready. That never brings about a positive result for either party involved.

What I've learned over the years is to accept what God is telling me, because it's truth. Another thing I've learned is to keep my mouth shut about it, until otherwise instructed. We wonder why we get a negative reaction from another child of God when we share something so wonderful that God has spoken, but we need to understand that He must prepare people to hear what we've heard, the same as He had to prepare US first. It's not any different than trying to show an algebra formula to someone who's learning long division right now. They'll consider what you're saying is complete nonsense, for they haven't even HEARD of algebra yet. God alone knows who's ready for the algebra lesson. He'll let you know when it's time to share.

chapter **44**
REVERSING THE SPLIT

The deepest healing that I experienced came at the least expected time. Joyce and I were meeting daily for prayer, whether it was Joyce coming down to my house, or me running up to hers. There were times though, when it just wasn't convenient for either of us to go out, and on those days we took full advantage of the telephone. This was one of those days. We began the prayer over the phone, the same way we began any other time, asking the Lord to show us what He wanted done for that particular day. Then we would simply surrender to the spirit prayer and wait for His instruction.

As we prayed, I became aware of a little girl standing just a few feet in front of me, in the spirit. She had her back to me. She had light blond hair, and was wearing a red dress with a large white yoke around the top. I told Joyce about the little girl I was watching, and she asked me if I knew who she was. Since she had her back to me and I couldn't see her face, I had no idea who it was that was standing there in the spirit. She appeared to be about the size of a three or four-year-old. We decided to stay with this, and see where it led, so we stayed in prayer while I continued to watch the little girl.

After watching for a few minutes, I casually mentioned to Joyce that an interesting thing about the little girl was her dress. The reason I found the dress interesting was because, as I commented to Joyce, I had had a dress just like that when I was a little girl. My mother had made it for me. Actually, she had made me two dresses like that, a red one, and a blue one just like it. This we found interesting, although that didn't help identify the little girl, nor had we found out yet why she had appeared.

We didn't seem to be getting anywhere, so finally Joyce suggested that I ask the little girl to turn around and look at me, since I was the one who was seeing her. I did just that, and to my surprise the little girl turned and I was finally able to see her face. Looking right at me now was the little girl that I had been, years ago. I asked the Lord why a much younger version of myself was standing in front of me, as though she were a separate person. He instructed me to speak to her.

The only thing I could think of to say was, "Hello". She remained still and solemn, staring at me blankly, as I watched her, fascinated, but she remained silent. I asked her now why she was there, and still she just looked at me in silence. Have you ever been introduced to a relative that you've never met before? You know who they are, but you really don't know them, so at the time of introduction you feel a little uncomfortable for you don't quite know how to approach this person. That's the kind of "uncomfortable" that I was feeling in this situation.

I questioned the Lord as to why I was to talk to her, since she wasn't answering, and He continued to instruct. "Call her by her name," was all He said.

Feeling more self-conscious now, I did what He told me by repeating, with my name this time, "Hello, Vicki". I really felt silly addressing a younger version of myself by my name. It felt weird, but I did it anyway, becoming even more curious by now as to what would happen. Again, I got no response, so I tried another approach with, "Vicki, why are you here?" When there was no response again, I became frustrated and turned my attention from the little girl to the Lord, wanting to know what was the purpose of this. His response to me was, "Call her by her nickname."

Again, I told Joyce what I had heard, and her response, naturally, was that I was just to do it. The problem that I had with this, I explained to her, was that Vicki IS my nickname, because my name is really Victoria. She then asked me if there was any other name anyone had ever called me when I was that young, and as I thought back, I recalled that my mother would sometimes call me "Vicki Girl". As a last resort, and feeling REALLY foolish now, I began again.

Determined to be obedient to the Spirit one more time before abandoning this pursuit, and this time using what I felt now was the "too cutesy" name my mother had used to greet me on occasion, I began again with, "Hello, Vicki Girl,..." and that was ALL I was going to be able to say for a while!

At the moment that I addressed the little girl by the name my mother had called me, it was as though a dam broke inside me, and great, horrible sobs came rushing up from deep within me. These sobs came so hard and so violently, they took my breath away. They couldn't be stopped, nor could they be subdued. There was so much emotional pain that accompanied those sobs, that I actually thought I would pass out. Searing, tearing, raw emotional pain was ALL I was experiencing now, and it completely overwhelmed me.

Minutes later, when I was able to compose myself enough to talk, we continued to pray through this experience. All the while this had been happening to me, I was aware of Joyce continuing to pray calmly in the spirit, and now I was able to join her again.

The Lord continued to instruct me concerning the little girl. "She needs you to hold her," He said. I wasn't sure how this was to be accomplished, but I opened my arms as I would to a child in the physical realm, in order to invite her to come for a hug, and she approached me cautiously. I wrapped my arms around her, pulling her close to me, and we became one person, united in spirit. I held her in spirit and prayed, while a quieter sobbing continued. I felt a powerfully protective love toward this little girl that I had just been introduced to, as I realized the depth of pain and terror that she had experienced.

Then the Lord spoke to me again. "Tell her the nightmare is over."

I told her the nightmare was over, and as I spoke these words, a new wave of hard sobs took over. The sobs were of weariness, pain, relief, and gratitude, and suddenly I was aware of this little girl's broken heart, and it broke my heart to realize how long she'd been ignored, and how helpless and lonely she had been for all these years. I reassured her again that the nightmare was over, and how sorry I was that no one had protected her, for she had been too little to handle the things that had happened to her so long ago, and assured her that it had never been her fault. I explained to her that although I'd not been able to protect her years ago, that now that I was grown up, God and I together would protect her from now on, and she would never have to experience the terror of the past again. I promised her that the Lord and I together would see to it that no one would hurt her any more. She would never be alone again, for I would never abandon her, now that I knew she existed. On and on the reassurance continued toward the little girl that I had been, until all the tears had been shed, and the fear and pain had finally subsided.

When this experience was finished, I found myself sitting alone now, with my arms wrapped across my chest, for the little girl had been pulled back inside of me, from where she had projected in the first place. We had been reunited, after all these years, and now I had acknowledged her, which was something that she had been craving all along. And I loved her with an overwhelming love.

The Lord continued to explain to me about the little girl I carried inside of me. He explained that she had been severely wounded by that age and had retreated into hiding because of those wounds. He told me that we all have an inner child, and that many have been hurt in just the same way that she had. Then, as an adult, I kept taking her through situations that continued to terrify her, without my even realizing that she was there. She had always been there, and He said that when I had felt the grip of inner fear, it was because the little girl inside was terrified again. I believe now that this is the root of the problem that many people call "Anxiety."

Have you met the child within you? Are you aware that the child is there? Was the child within you nurtured, appreciated and loved, or was that innocent, trusting little person crippled early in life? The wounded child is our wounded spirit. A wounded spirit becomes bitter and hateful. A loved child has no problem loving others, whereas a wounded child trusts no one. If we, as children, have been wounded by the adults we trusted, there was nothing we could do to stop it. However, as adults we ARE able, with the help of the Holy Spirit, to meet that wounded child, and by acknowledging, accepting, and loving them, we can finally undo all the damage that was done by others. It is then that the effects of childhood traumas are removed, and we begin to really love ourselves, and then, and only then, can we wholeheartedly extend that love to others. The Bible says that we are to love our neighbor as ourselves... and we DO.

The healing that I experienced that day, once begun, continued as an ongoing inner-therapy, for I came to find that the child in me, who was used to being mistreated and ignored, had to learn now to trust me to keep her safe, for I certainly hadn't done that all those years. There was no reason for her to trust me. There were times after that when circumstances would arise, that would cause me to feel panicked inside, but after I found out that I was carrying a frightened child within me, at the first sign of panic, I'd sit right down and wrap my arms around the little girl in me and begin to reassure her that everything was going to be all right. I would reaffirm to her that I wouldn't allow anyone to hurt her any more, until the panic would subside. These reassuring times occurred a few times over the next few months, but little by little she began to trust me, and the times of inner panic began to disappear. Inner pain and panic don't exist in my life any more.

God took the time to introduce me to a little girl in pain, and the love that I carry for that little girl will not allow me to take my life lightly any more. I can no longer say it doesn't matter if people mock me or mistreat me, for I've got a now-trusting little girl to protect, and it matters to me that she remain safe, for she is my innocence, and her innocence is my power. She's the "me" that God created.

The Bible says we are to become like little children, and I suspect that this is how we do it, by acknowledging our children within, and setting them free to live and enjoy life. No child should ever have to live in prison. Not yours, not mine, not anyone's.

chapter **45**

SQUEEZING THROUGH
THE KEYHOLE

Jesus said in Luke 7: 47 (Living Bible), "...but one who is forgiven little, shows little love." I always thought that had to be the reason I was so passionately in love with Him, because I had been forgiven so MUCH! I had made so many mistakes, and I had hurt so many people in my mission to self-destruct. When I met Him, and asked Him to take over my life, He just wiped the slate clean, and I began again as a brand-new person, whose faults and misconceptions were temporarily pushed aside, while I bathed in the love that He offered me. Who wouldn't fall in love with someone who could do that for them? Anyway, I so admired Him, that my natural desire was to become just like Him. I wanted to love the way He does, be strong the way He is, and be all-forgiving with others, the way He was with me.

I didn't know what would be involved in becoming like that, but I was willing to do whatever it took to become as much like Him as possible. The Bible states, in Romans 8:29 (Living Bible), "For from the very beginning God decided that those who came to Him-and all along He knew who would-should become like His Son, so that His Son would be the First, with many brothers." But how does He do that? He has planned a life for us that will, with His guidance, bring about that very thing, if we learn how to cooperate with His process. Now, before you think that just means the great evangelists, ministers, and prophets, but might not mean you, keep in mind that includes ALL of us who've come to Him, or are GOING to. We're all equal, and we're all born with traits that help equip us to do whatever God has purposed for us.

By all of us being equal, I don't mean we'll all be prophets, or preachers, or doctors, lawyers, or evangelists. I just mean that we're equally loved, and that we all have our contribution to make, for the betterment of us all.

If you're not feeling special because of where you are right now, you might be thinking like I used to think. There was a time when I thought that a doctor's profession would have to be more important than someone who just cleaned out the ditches alongside the road, until God showed me that if the man who cleaned out the ditches took pride in his work and did a good job, he was the one responsible for keeping the roads safe during bad weather. The clear roads, in turn, would enable the doctor to get to his patient in a life-threatening emergency. The ditch-cleaner's job, done well, was just as crucial to the saving of that patient, as the doctor was.

I said all that to say this. There is no one in God's family who is overlooked when it comes to the ability to become like Jesus. In earlier years I had always looked at other people as more important than me, smarter than me, and more special than me. It took God some serious work with me to convince me otherwise, but He finally made me understand that I, too, was important in His Plan. I'm not MORE important than anyone else, but I am AS important as anyone else, the same as you.

I was having a problem forgiving again. I just couldn't imagine why people were sometimes so rotten toward me. I'd be doing the best I knew how to do, thinking that all was going well, then BAM! When I'd least expect it, someone would come along and do something or say something so hurtful, that I'd go into another state of emotional shock. Ever have that happen? I was fed up with the blows I would take from others, and I was just having a hard time figuring WHY I had to keep forgiving these things. After all, all I wanted was to love the people around me, but sometimes the people around me were downright vicious.

I know the old saying, "Jesus suffered, too," but you know, sometimes that just doesn't help to know that. It doesn't take the pain away, just knowing that someone else has suffered pain. If I have a broken leg, it doesn't help me to look across the emergency room and see someone else with a broken leg. You may feel badly for them, too, but it's just not fixing your leg. You need more, and you know it.

So here I was, wounded again, and tired of it. I was tired of people around me being rotten, and tired of being made fun of because I had come to God. I knew we were supposed to be forgiving, but forgiving these people over and over again didn't seem to be making much of a difference that I could see. Now I would do what I always had to do for comfort. I ran to my best friend. I had developed the habit of going to the Lord with everything, good or bad. He was my best friend in the whole world, and I didn't play any pious games with Him. I talked to Him like I would talk to anyone else, and now I was disgusted, and I told Him so. I vented. I mean, I really VENTED!

I told him everything I thought about the uselessness of forgiving people who just were going to insist on being jerks, no matter what! I ranted and raved my anger to God, until I had gotten it all out, and then, and only then, was I willing to hear what He had to say. There had to be some kind of very good reason for me to be going through these things, over and over, I had informed Him, and I would have to know the reason now, or I just wasn't playing this forgiveness game any more. Enter: another vision.

Jesus was now standing right in front of me. He wasn't angry that I had vented. He was the same as always, full of love, compassion, strength, and peace. There was a closed door in a doorframe between us, but I could see through the door, for it was as clear as glass. There were no walls, just a door in a doorframe. He stood on one side of the door, looking at me, while I stood on the other side of the door, looking at Him. He said "What do you want more than anything else?"

There was no doubt what I wanted, standing there looking at the most magnificent love that I'd ever known. "I want to be able to be like You, Lord," was all I had to say, for nothing else mattered in His presence.

"Come where I am, and you will be."

"But how do I come where YOU are, Lord? Don't I have to die to be where You are?"

"Come through this door, and you will be like me." he said softly.
I was thrilled! The only place I ever wanted to be was where
He was. I reached for the doorknob to open the door, only to find
that there was none. "Lord," I said startled, "there's no doorknob.
I can't open the door!"

Now He said, "You must come through this door, if you want
to be like me."

Determined to get where I needed to be, I started pushing on
the door. Maybe, I was hoping, it would just swing open. I pushed
from all angles, but the door wasn't budging.

"Lord!" I said, getting frustrated with the situation, "is this
some kind of joke? You tell me to come through a door that
has no way to come through it? There's no doorknob, and it's as
though the door's been super-glued to the frame. There's no WAY
to come through this door."

"There IS a way to come through." He answered. "Look closer."

As I looked at the door again, my vision now focused on a
keyhole. I hadn't noticed it before. I continued to scrutinize every
inch of that door, and even tried pushing on it a time or two again,
with no luck, but then my attention was brought back to the keyhole. My excitement at the prospect of coming through the door
was now turning to despair. "Lord, I can't come through," I said
sadly, "there's nothing here but a little keyhole."

"Then come through there" was His response.

"You know I can't fit through there!" I couldn't believe He had
said such a thing.

"What would happen if you tried?" he asked me.

"Nothing would happen." I replied. "There's no part of me
that could possibly get through there. Well, my spirit, maybe, but
nothing else."

"Exactly," said the Lord. "That's the point. In order to become
like me, you must leave behind all that you are, all of your old
structure, and even leave all of your old thoughts behind, for they
won't fit through, either. Spirit is all that CAN come through
this door. If you desire to come through, you must leave all that
behind. You have already begun this journey, from the moment
you asked to be like me. You've prayed to receive my thoughts to

replace your own, and, upon receiving, you've left the old behind. Each time you've done this, you've come through just a little more, replacing physical knowledge with spirit knowledge. The transition to the Christ life is like a journey through the keyhole. Difficult, but not impossible. I know the desire of your heart, and it is to go through the transition, and there have been times on this journey when you've gotten stuck because of your own beliefs, which were flesh, and the inability to let go of them. It is in these times that I've sent someone your way to give you a helping hand."

With that, a new vision appeared, one that made me laugh out loud. I saw the keyhole, and I saw a much tinier version of myself part way through, and I was definitely stuck. Couldn't move an inch! Then, as I watched, I saw the very person that I was angry with this time, and he had in his hands a giant mallet. As I struggled in my stuck position, the man stopped, saw my predicament, and gave me such a whack with that mallet, that it drove me through the keyhole just a little further, ripping some flesh off in the process. Oh, it wasn't a bloody, gory scene at all. It was just plain hilarious!

My desire to be on the other side of that door was much stronger than my anger now about whatever means it would take to get me to my destination. I continued to talk with the Lord about how this process worked, as I laughed about the body stuck in the keyhole. He explained to me that the only thing that would be able to come through was anything that was in total agreement with God. Every time I ran into a wrong concept in me that held up my progress, it had to be removed, if I were to successfully get to the other side.

A few times, He said, I had held on tightly to something I had been taught, about myself , life, or even about God, and believed to be true, but if it weren't pure truth, it had to be stripped. The works of the flesh had to go. Oops, I'm a little further through! All pre-conceived notions had to be destroyed. Yep, a little further! All dependence on anything but God to have my needs met... Uh, Oh,! Get the mallet! I couldn't do anything but laugh at the image God had given me concerning this transformation process. I ended up that day, not only losing the anger concerning my last wound, but joyously blessing the one who had hurt me. All he had really done was strip me of a little more of what needed to be removed, for me to get on with my journey through the keyhole.

I wasn't having a problem forgiving anyone NOW. As a matter of fact, quite the opposite occurred. I began looking back at the people who had hurt me since I'd come to know the Lord, and I started to see the pattern. I would get hurt, I'd run to the Lord for help, and we would spend time together while He instructed me in things I hadn't understood before. It was astonishing to me to realize just how much my concepts had been changed during those times, and although I had forgiven people in the past who had hurt me, I now found myself moving beyond just forgiving, to now praying blessings all over these people, for the part they were playing in getting me through. I chuckled to myself because of what I had just learned, and wondered if any of them had any idea when they "struck" me, what they had actually done for me. Although they had wounded my pride, my ego, my self, which needed to be removed anyway, they had blessed me beyond measure, for they had helped me to get just a little closer to the other side of that door, into pure knowledge of God, where Jesus is, and where I truly wanted to be.

Because of what God taught me about going through the keyhole, I now have a completely different concept of Jesus on the cross. I used to think of Him as sadly saying "Father forgive them, for they know not what they do.", (Luke 23, KJV) and I thought that He had forgiven them, simply because it was the right thing to do. I also had the idea that He'd forgiven them with a sense of feeling badly about them, because they just couldn't see who He was, and because they had hurt Him so much. But I don't see it that way any more, because I have a suspicion that He knew about the keyhole too, and He knew much more about what was happening to Him than we would understand for a very long time.

I see Him now, the Victorious One, spirit lifted in joy to God the Father, and shouting in that joy, although His physical voice would have been reduced to a mere whisper by now, "Whatever you do, Father, don't hold anything against them for this, for they have no idea what they've just done for me, and for the people of this world!" And I believe that when He said "Into Thy hands I commend my spirit"(Luke 23, KJV), He knew that He had completed His mission, all flesh had been destroyed and He was coming through the keyhole at last. There was nothing to look forward to now but resurrection power! He did all that He did, as an example for us to follow.

We can cooperate with God in this life, even to the death of everything we are, meaning allowing Him to strip us of everything in us that is US and not Him, and experience that resurrection power of God that comes from the sometimes painful, yet totally transforming, journey through the keyhole.

chapter **46**
REVISITING HELL

I've already described the fear I had of my father, but as I became a teenager, the fear had turned to hatred. I wanted him dead. I wanted him gone. He finally left, but that didn't happen until I was fifteen years old, so deep patterns of fear and hatred had already been set in me. Over the years I would hear things about him. I heard that he had married the woman he had left with, and as time passed, I had heard that they had children, a boy and a girl. I would wonder from time to time how he treated them, but there was no way of knowing, since I never knew where they were. It's not that I would have looked him up, because any time I ever heard him mentioned in conversation, I felt the same repulsion that I always had.

There were times when I worried, especially about the daughter, but these people were not real to me, and they were far away, and all I knew was that I was safe from him. Sometimes there would be rumors that he had been forced to move again because of being in trouble with neighbors, because of "incidents" with their children, but these were stories that got passed around, and who knew if they were true. I suspected they were.

Seventeen years had passed since I had last seen him, and the last I'd heard, he and his family had moved to a town a little over an hour from where I lived. I had no desire to know exactly where.

During one of those very unnerving times with my second husband, who was drinking heavily and being especially cruel, I kept asking God for mercy. I needed a break from this barrage of name-calling accusations, and insanity that had surrounded me again, as if to swallow me up completely. I had learned that if you needed something in your life, you had to first give that very 'something' that you needed. You had to give love, in order to receive it, and you had to give encouragement, to be encouraged, so I surmised that I would have to give mercy in order to receive mercy.

I knew I needed a large dose of mercy and kindness at this point, so I looked for somewhere to bestow the same. As I prayed about where to show mercy, my dad came to mind. It would take a lot for me to be merciful and kind to him. As far as I was concerned, that would be above and beyond the call of duty, even for a born-again child of God. Call it a spiritual experiment if you like, but I knew I had to try.

Once my mind was made up that I was going to look him up, it was easy enough to find him. All I had to do was stop at the little gas station in that town and ask, and I was given directions to his house. When I got there, I pulled into the driveway, and decided to back out again, in order to turn around and park my car in front of the house. I had backed out of the drive and turned my car and was now sitting broadside across the entrance to the drive, ready to shift gears and move forward a little, when I spotted a teenage girl coming out the side door, keys in hand, briskly walking toward a car that was parked by the house. She was a very pretty blond-haired girl, and I thought to myself that this had to be his daughter. I just sat there for a moment, unnoticed and curious, while I watched her go to the car. Then she stopped and turned around, but still didn't seem to have noticed me. I was partially hidden, I guess, by some bushes.

She started to walk slowly back toward the porch, and I could tell someone was talking to her from inside because of the way her head tilted, listening. Then, as she approached the porch, the screen door opened, and a man stepped out. Was this my dad? He was saying something to her, and I caught my breath as she stepped back a little from him, as if not to get too close. I recognized that move immediately. I had done that around my father all my life. It's an instinctive hedging that you see an animal make when it senses danger. "Oh, God!" I thought, "she's afraid of him, too." I made a mental note of this, and pulled my car forward.

I remained in my car as the girl got into her car and pulled out. I sat watching the man as he now came walking toward my car, but I didn't recognize this man. I studied him intently as he approached, but by the time he got to my car, I thought I must be at the wrong house, although I was sure I had gotten the directions right. The man stepped up to my car, looked right at me and said, "Can I help you with something?"

"Are you…?" I had stated my dad's full name, not sure who this man was. I studied his face closely, looking for anything familiar, still not sure.

"Yes, that's me. Can I help you with something?" he repeated, and I now realized that this really was the man that I had feared all of my life. And now here he stood, right in front of me, and I wasn't afraid. "Why, he's just a little old man now" I thought. "He couldn't possibly hurt me any more."

"Do you know who I am?" I asked quietly.

"No, I don't believe I do." he commented, matter-of-factly.

"My name's Vicki. Do you know who I am?"

He looked at me for a moment, then said, "Nope, I'm afraid I don't. Should I know you?"

"I'm your daughter," I said, waiting for any kind of reaction.

"Who did you say you are?" he asked again, leaning a little closer to the car, this time studying my face.

"My name is Vicki. I'm your daughter. Do you remember me?"

He stood there for a minute, looking at me blankly, before it finally dawned on him who I was.

"Oh, yes! Well, come in, come in!"

I got out of the car, and as he ushered me toward his house, a woman came out the front door. For the first time in my life I heard this man speak my name, as he introduced me to his wife. They were both welcoming, and I was curiously surprised. I really didn't know what to talk to them about, so I asked questions about aunts and uncles and cousins, and they filled me in on where everyone was, and what they were doing. We sat there and talked for about a half-hour, when there was a bang of the screen door, and a young, blond-haired boy in his late teens walked in.

He was slender. He was heading straight through the living room where we sat, without looking at anyone, when my father told him to wait a minute, there was someone there he wanted him to meet. He had to tell him twice, to get him to stop, and when this young man turned around to look at my father, I saw pure hatred in his eyes. He obediently suffered through the introduction, said "Hello", and left the room. My heart broke for him right then, as I wondered what kind of a nightmare he had lived in with this man.

I guess I had believed that they probably had a normal family life, because I thought for years that I was the cause of all my problems, because I was just a freak of some sort, and I had entertained the thought that my dad was happier with his other family, and maybe he was better with this family than he'd been with ours. Although I had despised him, and had occasionally worried what he might be like with his other kids, I had told myself that they were probably fine, and it was just me that had had a weird life. But now I was seeing evidence that what I had told myself might not be true. At that moment these young people became very real to me, and I silently vowed that someday I would find a way to help them both, if they would let me. I became weary now of the small talk and told them that it was time I got going back home. They talked about coming to visit sometime, so I told them where I lived.

As they walked outside with me, and stood on the sidewalk in front of their house, I said my goodbyes, and then did something totally out of context for me. I kissed my dad on the cheek and said "Bye, Dad, I love you". I had never done that before. It felt odd saying that to him, because I didn't love him. I didn't even know him. I thought about this strange thing I had done all the way home. And then I knew why I had said it. It was my way of saying, "I survived, and you're forgiven", to a man who hadn't cared if I'd survived, and had never asked to be forgiven.

It wasn't long after that that my dad, his wife, and my half-sister came to visit one evening. It was strained for me, because these people were strangers. My half-sister was my daughter's age, and very polite and quiet. They visited for the evening, then headed home. I had been nervous about them, so I remained an observer. I did, however, call after that to wish my dad a happy Father's Day.

Months later, or longer, my dad showed up at my house again, this time with his sister who had come from a southern state to visit. I thoroughly enjoyed this woman, but I had liked her as a child. Toward the end of this visit, my aunt had mentioned that she played the piano. I was storing my mother's organ in another room of the house, and I asked her if she'd play something for us. She showed an amazing talent, as she rattled off some country music, but soon she settled into some hymns. I stood by her, enjoying the music, and hadn't noticed that my dad and my husband had left the room. Startled, I walked into the next room, thinking they must have gone back to the kitchen, but when I came around the corner of the next room, there they stood, in a conspiratorial huddle, with my father telling an obscene joke to my husband. The moment that I realized what that topic of conversation was, I froze. I silently vowed that I would never permit this man in my house again. He hadn't changed, and I was sickened. I threw away his phone number, knowing that I would never call him again.

I didn't see him again for another few years, until he showed up with his wife at my mother's funeral. I was shocked that he had come, but I walked over to him to acknowledge his presence. I did this simply because I felt it was the right thing to do. We stood there talking politely for a few minutes, when all of a sudden, I stepped back from him, repulsed, and very aware of that same diabolical presence within him. Sickened again, I could no longer talk to him, so I politely made my exit from the conversation, and found my way to the bathroom. I was badly shaken inside, and I knew that something evil in this man had just touched my spirit. I quickly composed myself, and returned to the guests at the funeral. There was no way that I could possibly tolerate the twisted entity that lived inside this man. Surely this would be the last time I'd ever have to see him.

chapter 47
FULL CIRCLE

A couple of years ago, I was privileged to have an experience that far exceeded my understanding of being healed. It was an experience that completed my own inner healing in a way I would never have imagined. I was permitted to do something that I now call going "full circle".

An interesting message had been given while Joyce and I were together. We had assumed it was for her, since she's the one who had heard it. The message was "You will go to Pittsburgh within the next few days. You will not WANT to go, but you will HAVE to go." It turned out the message was for me.

I was awakened a couple of days later by my phone ringing. I got up and answered it, to hear a woman asking me how I was, and telling me that she had thought she'd better call me. I had said I was fine when she asked, but since I wasn't really awake yet, I focused intently on the voice, trying to identify this woman. It wasn't working. I had to interrupt her to ask who was calling. She told me her first name in a tone that implied I should have known this. I immediately started flipping through the rolodex in my mind, still trying to pinpoint who this was that was talking to me in such a familiar tone.

Having no luck identifying my caller, I asked again, embarrassed this time. When she fully explained who she was, I lost the embarrassment. I forgave myself immediately for not recognizing the voice of my step-mother. Since I had only met her a couple of times, and hadn't heard her voice in years, it stood to reason I wouldn't recognize it now.

She started now to tell me that my father had suffered a stroke, and was in a hospital in Pittsburgh. I had no desire to see my dad whatsoever, since he had caused so much pain in my life, but I was shocked at the desire that suddenly welled up in me to get to know my step-mother. The desire was so strong, that I know I shocked her when I said I would come and get her and take her to see him, when she didn't really need someone to take her. She was perfectly capable of getting there herself. I insisted, however, and the arrangement was made.. Having to see my dad, however disagreeable this might be, wasn't going to deter me from spending the day with this woman that I suddenly needed to know.

I was up early, two days later, to go get my step-mother, and take her to Pittsburgh. I couldn't imagine why I was so curious about a woman that I'd never known, but it was that curiosity that forced me that day to go to see my dad again. It made no sense, but that driving force got me to where I had to be. God definitely had a plan for THIS day. She and I chatted pleasantly as we headed for the hospital. I was finding that she was a much more outgoing person than my mother had been, so I surmised that this would have been an attraction to my dad.

We arrived at the hospital before lunch, and she led me to my dad's room. He didn't know me again, so I had to be re-introduced to him. They talked about what the doctor had said, and how he was progressing. He asked about my husband, so I filled him in on what he was doing with his time. While the three of us talked, my step-mother occupying a chair on one side of dad's bed, while I had claimed a chair at the foot of the bed, I watched this elderly man, talking like anyone else, with a little humor thrown into his conversation from time to time. There was nothing unusual in this.

At one point, though, when my step-mother was talking to a nurse who had entered the room, I watched as the man in the bed seemed to change. He was now looking at his wife in the same way that a puzzled child would look to his mother to find out what to do next. He was studying her through innocent, little-boy eyes, as if awaiting instructions. His eyes were full of childlike wonder. I was startled by this, not quite understanding why I was seeing it, but fully aware that I was. I was seeing a vulnerability in this terrifying man, that touched my heart as I realized that we are all just little children inside. I'm such a studier of people anyway, and my habit of taking mental notes didn't get overlooked that day concerning this "little boy" being revealed to me.

The next phase of this experience would not be so pleasant. Casual conversation continued, and my dad had returned to being his normal self. At one point in the conversation, my step-mother had turned toward me to tell me something, but as I listened, I exercised my life-long habit of always keeping a watchful eye on my father. While she was turned to me, I saw him beginning to watch her carefully, and then it began.

With her totally oblivious to him for the moment, he kept glancing back at her to make sure she wasn't able to see what he was doing, but I knew that look, and I knew what he was going to do. I had known that look all my life. I knew he was pulling aside his hospital gown to expose his unclothed body. My step-mother and I sat low enough by the bed to be able to see only his elevated head and chest, but my spirit had gone into red alert. "OH, NO!" I was screaming inside, "don't do it, don't do it, DON'T DO THIS!" Too late. I sat frozen. My stomach twisted into a hard knot.

This man now turned his head to look straight at me. The change that took place on his face and in his eyes sent a chill up my spine, while the hair on the back of my neck stood straight up. My step-mother continued to chatter while I sat staring into eyes that had become glazed, glaring slits in this now contorted face. I have never witnessed such an intensely evil hatred as I saw in those eyes that day. His face had changed to a distorted version of the face that had been there before, and I knew beyond a shadow of a doubt that I was staring into the eyes of something so hideous that it couldn't be described.

I was face to face now with that vile entity that had been my enemy since birth. There sat that fiercely twisted and hateful spirit, glaring at me, despising me, and challenging me to do anything about this. I turned my eyes away from this creature, for I knew this was no longer the man we had come to visit, but something too frightening for me to look at. This was the spirit that had lived in this man for years, and it was terrifying. I couldn't believe that I was paralyzed with fear again, and that it went beyond fear to terror. I had known this terror of this man as a child, but I was a grown woman now, having experienced years of spiritual warfare, and here I sat, unable to move in the presence of something that vile.

A nurse came into the room right then, smiled, and casually commented on this man being uncovered, as though it had been an accident. And just as casually, she put his gown back where it belonged. As she rearranged his sheets, I was silently screaming to her to wake up! I was wordlessly screaming to her that his being uncovered was not an accident, but a deliberate act. Couldn't she SEE that? She needed to alert the other nurses as to what they were dealing with! There was such an intensity in my spirit-to-spirit message to her that it hit target.

While she was covering him and being pleasant, as nurses are, her facial expression suddenly changed as though she had just been struck. She was no longer smiling, but sternly alert. I knew in my spirit that the message I was silently screaming to her had been received. Somehow It had gotten through to her. I knew it had, because I saw her receive it. I felt the release and the relief, knowing that my alert message had been successfully transferred.

They came to get him after that to move him to another room that they had been preparing for him, and of course he had changed back again to his harmless-little-old-man image. I recovered again, as they removed him from the room, and we waited until he was settled on the next floor, and went there to say goodbye for the day. It was time for us to go. He was asleep when we went into the new room, and I was glad, for now I didn't have to deal with him. I didn't dwell on what I had witnessed, I was just happy to leave.

Pleasant chatting took place again while I drove my stepmother home, but when I got her home, and pulled out again to start the hour-and-a-half journey to my house, I began talking to the Lord about what I had witnessed. I had seen the innocence of this man's childlike spirit, and I had seen the outward man that was portrayed to the world. I had also seen the foul spirit that could push him aside and take him over whenever it pleased. This was a man possessed by something much more powerful than he was. What an amazing day I'd had, and all I had thought was that I was going to get to know my step-mother.

When I got home, I called my prayer partner to tell her what all had happened, but there was no prayer at this time concerning any of it. Just a passing on of information.

It wasn't until early the following afternoon, while I was sitting at my computer, that the intercession for this man began. I hadn't been able to shake off the image of the little boy I'd seen in my father's eyes the day before. It had haunted me all morning. When the prayer came, it came swiftly, and with such compassion that I was amazed. God had permitted me to see that vile, hateful spirit in that man, but He had also permitted me to see the innocent child inside. It was the child inside the man that I began to pray for. I realized that this child was a victim also, and suddenly I couldn't imagine the amount of torment this little boy had lived in all these years.

I ended up that afternoon, draped across my desk, begging for mercy for this little boy. The very mercy that I had decided to show this man years ago, was finally being really shown in prayer, while I beseeched God with everything in me to set this child free from this hideous influence before he left this world. Tears flowed freely as I begged God for mercy for this man. I doubt that I would have been able to do this, but God had shown me a part of the man that had to be saved from this creature that had used him for years. I knew no one would deliberately want to live like this, and I knew the frightened little boy inside of him had no power over it, and so I begged for God to intervene with His mercy.

I called my prayer partner to tell her what was happening, and she arrived in as little time as it took for her to drive to my house. We went to war on my dad's behalf that day, and it was powerful. We could not give up until it was finished. It took the rest of the afternoon in intense prayer, following the instructions of the Holy Spirit, but it was finally finished, and we both knew he was free.

I went to see him one more time after that, because of the drawing of the spirit, only to find no one home, although I knew he had been released from that hospital only days after I had been there. I drove around that little town for a while, and went back to the house again. There was still no one home. There was no use staying around, so I left again with the intention of going home, but I couldn't seem to leave this little town. Feeling somewhat foolish by now, I returned to the house for the third time. This time I found my step-mother just pulling into her driveway. She said my dad had been home, but was now in the nursing home in town, because he had gotten sick again, and had been moved to the nursing home following another hospital visit.

I drove to the nursing home. When I found him, he was sitting in a wheelchair in his room. He knew me this time, and I stayed in the room for quite a while talking with him. He was grouchy, and funny, and pleasant, all at the same time, and I chuckled many times at his funny way of saying things.

That day was the first time I was ever around this man that I had no hesitation in talking to him, nor did it bother me to be near him. What I found this time was a glorious absence of evil. There was nothing in the room but peace, and I knew now that I'd had to come, to confirm that the prayer had set him free. There was no evidence whatsoever of the vile spirit that had been present with him before. No red alerts, no nervousness of any kind, just peace. When I was leaving the nursing home that night, I kissed him on the forehead and said, "Bye, Dad. I love you". When I had said it before, I had said that as a way of saying "I forgive you". This time was different. This time when I said "I love you", I actually meant it, not as a daughter would love a father, because I'd never known him that way. I honestly loved him as a fellow human being, a trapped little boy, who had desperately needed God's help, the same as me.

During his funeral a couple of weeks later, the minister talked about how he had asked my dad so many times if he could pray with him, and how my dad would answer with an emphatic NO! But he also mentioned that, although he hadn't known what had changed all that, the last time he had seen him he had asked again if he could pray with him, and to his surprise, my dad had said YES! I smiled. I knew what had changed him. God had set him free from that very thing that stood in the way of my dad ever asking for

God. No one could get past that other spirit to find out that the child inside had always wanted God. Children always do.

When I met the child inside of me, and experienced that deepest healing, I had thought that there was no further a person could go in that respect. I had experienced healing down into the very core of who I am. I had thought that there could be nothing greater than this. Then, thanks to God and a man who had terrified me all my life, I learned of a step beyond healing, a step so rewarding that it's hard to put into words.

It's a wonderful thing to be freed from a personal hell, in which you were terrorized by other citizens of that condition, but even more wonderful to be sent back, free to free the others. That is an honor beyond anything I can describe. That's what I've come to call going "full circle", when you're healed enough to circle back and rescue those you left behind in the hell that you escaped from.

chapter 48
INTIMACY

Would you send someone else into your bedroom to spend time with your marriage partner, then wait anxiously for that person to return and tell you what your partner said during that time of intimacy? Of course not! You would spend the time with your partner yourself, and the intimate conversation that takes place between the two of you is only for your ears. We all crave that intimate relationship with the Lord, for that's what we're made for. It's a marriage relationship.

Have you ever wondered why people seem to become "luke-warm" in their relationship with God, when knowing Him should have become more and more exciting as time went on? What happens to that excitement that is experienced when we first meet Him? Many people have not been taught enough about that intimacy to know how to enter into it. We won't pursue a deeper relationship with God if we believe that He only talks to the pastors and the preachers and the evangelists.

We enter into the intimacy when we stay in prayer and push past all the things we have been taught by others, and past all the cares of this life, to get to the place where nothing exists but us and the Lord. We have no desire to hear from anyone but Him, nor do we have a desire to be interrupted during this time. The only way I've found to get into this type of intimacy is to pray "in the spirit" and allow the Holy Spirit to usher me into this intimate place with the Lord. There's a joy in spending time with others who are like-minded, but there is NOTHING more fulfilling than spending your own intimate time with Him. It only adds to your joy when you assemble together with others, and have something wonderful to share because of the things he has taught you Himself.

We are all unique in the way we are made, and we each have a specific path to walk, but how will we ever know each step to take, if we don't find out from the Lord? We all want to be used by God to fulfill our own purpose, and we will when we find out what our individual instructions are. How can someone else tell me how to walk my path, when that someone else has a path of their own that they are receiving instructions about? Their path and mine are not the same.

We are to assemble ourselves together, but that is not the whole relationship. The Bible refers in Second John 2: 27 to the fact that we no longer need to be taught by men, now that we have the Holy Spirit. We need to be taught by the Holy Spirit, and come together for worship and sharing. We are empowered by the intimacy with the Lord, and we are built up in faith by the assembling together with the body. I've heard many sermons over the years, and they've been helpful, but I can't tell you too many specifics about any of them, just that they helped build my faith. What I CAN tell you about though, is anything God Himself has taught me. What HE has taught me is mine forever. There is no storm on Earth that can shake my faith in what He has given me personally.

We can't stay babies forever, and have to run to the pastor every time we have a question. Well, we can, but doesn't it stand to reason that we should be growing up to learn how to get the answers ourselves?

When we begin to go to school, do we learn to go to the teacher and ask what the answer is to every math problem? No, we don't, and that's because the teacher is there to teach you the formulas that will enable you get your own answers. The teacher is at the head of the classroom to equip you with whatever you need, so that you can move on into your own life successfully. The greatest teacher is the one who sees to it that you no longer need a teacher.

This is also the function of a spiritual teacher. The teacher is there only to equip you with the formulas and tools to help you to get to God for your own answers. The only teacher that you will ALWAYS have need of is the Holy Spirit. If men are in pulpits, and they're teaching you to come to them, rather than equipping you to go to God, then you need to be wary of them. It is all-to-easy for men to get caught up in the importance of their role, and too easy for them to take on too much responsibility for your life. The responsibility of the minister, or teacher, is simply to equip you to do it yourself, with God. We need to stop burdening these men with our everyday problems, and learn to come to God ourselves. We need to free these teachers to teach babies the formulas of God's principals, and stop sitting in the pews wanting always to be taught. The churches are the classrooms, and too many of us have become professional students, when we should by now be teaching in classrooms of our own.

There are many who will remain in their places in the church they were raised in, because that's where God has stationed them. There are others who will be moved, in order to be positioned elsewhere, but how will we know where we're to be, if we're not in communication with Him?

In Matthew 4:19 (KJV), Jesus said, "Follow me, and I will make you fishers of men." It was the same as saying, "Do what I do" or "Follow my example". And what exactly WAS the example He set before us to follow? He would get away from the people to get in touch with the Father, and receive instructions from Him to walk the path that the Father had for Him to walk. He was our example of an intimate relationship with the Father. He was the only one who could fulfill His very unique purpose. Are we following His example of communion with the Father to get OUR instructions for our OWN very unique purpose? Our purpose may not be as dramatic as His, but it is none-the-less important that we fulfill our role, the same as He had to fulfill His. He said that He didn't do anything on His own, but only what He saw the Father doing. He was looking into another realm to see what was the Father's will. Do we stay in prayer to see what the Father shows us that He wants US to do? Or are our spiritual eyes still closed? We need to have them opened. God has things in the spirit that He will show us to do in order for us to fulfill OUR purpose, too!

Jesus said in Matt.12:48-50,(KJV) "Who is my mother? Who are my brothers? These are my mother and brothers. Anyone who does God's will is my brother, and my sister, and my mother". (Notice, He said GOD'S will, not our own!) God's will for us is that we live according to His principles, but He also has specific instructions for us as well. Are we assuming that we know His purpose for us, or do we REALLY know what He has in store for us, like Jesus did?

We all learn from spending time together. Bonds of love are nurtured when we come together and share the love of God with one another, but the marriage relationship will always be the same ...one-on-one. Don't neglect the marriage for the sake of the children, for when it comes right down to it, spiritual children will do the same as earthly children. They will grow up and leave you in order to fulfill their role in life, if they've been raised properly. We don't want an "empty-nest syndrome" on our hands when it comes to the marriage with the Lord. We don't want to find the marriage relationship lacking when everyone else has gone away. The best way to raise up spiritual children is the same best way to raise up our earthly children, by showing them what's most important always, and that's an intimate love relationship with God. This is not taught with words, but it is shown by example.

I was in a meeting in someone's house once, and the teacher for the day led everyone in prayer before we left. The woman had been talking about how we raise our children, and how sometimes we like to keep them dependent on us for way too long, and how we need to cut the apron strings that our children are tied to, and let them grow up, so they can become strong on their own, and not be dependent on us forever. When she lead us in prayer, she said we were to ask the Lord to show us the apron strings that needed to be cut. I asked, but there were none. It was then that I realized how much I had NOT wanted my children to always be dependent on me. I was the one who wanted them to learn to tie their OWN shoestrings, and get their OWN drinks of water. I began to tell the Lord what a horrible mother I was, because I didn't WANT them to stay babies, like other mothers did.

Just about the time I began apologizing for being a bad mother again, He surprised me with an interruption to my self-condemning. He said I was mistaken about the criticism, for I was being exactly how He needed me to be. He told me that this trait of wanting the children to grow up, rather than stay babies, would be useful in the raising of His children, for this was His attitude also. He wants us to grow up, not sit around being spoon-fed by others all our lives. We need to grow up and become strong in order to help feed the new babies ourselves. They're coming, you know, and lots of them! Then we need to know when to let go, and watch them begin to walk on their own. They'll thank us for this someday, as they're entering into their own intimate relationship with God to fulfill their own unique purpose.

The End...

Or a New Beginning.

You Decide.

CPSIA information can be obtained
at www.ICGtesting.com
Printed in the USA
BVHW041851010521
606241BV00007B/10

9 781632 216670